At Issue

Migrant Workers

Other Books in the At Issue Series:

At Issue

Migrant Workers

Roman Espejo, Book Editor

GREENHAVEN PRESS
A part of Gale, Cengage Learning

GALE
CENGAGE Learning·

Farmington Hills, Mich • San Francisco • New York • Waterville, Maine
Meriden, Conn • Mason, Ohio • Chicago

Patricia Coryell, *Vice President & Publisher, New Products & GVRL*
Douglas Dentino, *Manager, New Products*
Judy Galens, *Acquisitions Editor*

For more information, contact:
Greenhaven Press
27500 Drake Rd.
Farmington Hills, MI 48331-3535
Or you can visit our Internet site at gale.cengage.com

For product information and technology assistance, contact us at

Gale Customer Support, 1-800-877-4253
For permission to use material from this text or product, submit all requests online at www.cengage.com/permissions

Further permissions questions can be emailed to permissionrequest@cengage.com

Articles in Greenhaven Press anthologies are often edited for length to meet page requirements. In addition, original titles of these works are changed to clearly present the main thesis and to explicitly indicate the author's opinion. Every effort is made to ensure that Greenhaven Press accurately reflects the original intent of the authors. Every effort has been made to trace the owners of copyrighted material.

Cover image © Images.com/Corbis.

LIBRARY OF CONGRESS CATALOGING-IN-PUBLICATION DATA

Migrant workers / Roman Espejo, book editor.
      pages cm. -- (At issue)
   Includes bibliographical references and index.
   ISBN 978-0-7377-7177-0 (hardcover) -- ISBN 978-0-7377-7178-7 (pbk.)
   1. Foreign workers--United States. 2. Migrant agricultural laborers--United States. 3. Immigrants--Employment--United States. 4. Labor market--United States. I. Espejo, Roman, 1977-
      HD8081.A5M54 2015
      331.5'440973--dc23
                                                            2014032518

Printed in the United States of America
   2 3 4 5 6   19 18 17 16 15

Contents

Introduction

In 2013, it was reported that more than 100 million out of the world's 214 million migrant workers were women, surpassing men in some areas. Aside from financially supporting their households, women go abroad to work for various reasons. According to Babatunde Osotimehin, executive director of the United Nations Population Fund (UNFPA), many women "leave their homes in search of more open societies, to get out of a bad marriage, or to escape all forms of discrimination and gender-based violence, political conflicts, and cultural constraints."[1] Experts note, however, that many of these women encounter varying degrees of sexism in their host countries, affecting the jobs that are available to them. "Reproducing patterns of gender inequality, at [their] destination they tend to find work in traditionally female-dominated occupations such as domestic work,"[2] maintains the International Labour Organization (ILO), which is a specialized agency of the United Nations.

The growing number of women from developing countries who leave their families to become nannies, housekeepers, and cooks for other families has entered the global discussion. "The links between domestic work and female international labour migration is well established," the ILO contends. "The growing demand of households for domestic services is considered to be one of the main triggers of the feminization of labour migration which we have witnessed in past decades."[3] While many are fairly treated and provide

---

1. Quoted in Thalif Deen, "Over 100 Million Women Lead Migrant Workers Worldwide," Inter Press Service, April 30, 2013. http://www.ipsnews.net/2013/04/over-100-million-women-lead-migrant-workers-worldwide.
2. International Labour Organization, "Migrant Domestic Workers," accessed June 28, 2014. http://www.ilo.org/global/topics/labour-migration/policy-areas/migrant-domestic-workers/lang--en/index.htm.
3. Ibid.

valuable services, domestic migrant workers are at special risk of abuse and injustice, the agency warns. "Their vulnerabilities are often linked to precarious recruitment processes (including passport and contract substitution as well as charging of excessive fees), the absence of adapted assistance and protection mechanisms, the social and cultural isolation they can face at the destination due to language and cultural differences, lack of advance and accurate information on terms and conditions of employment, absence of labour law coverage and/or enforcement in the country of destination, and restrictions on freedom of movement and association, among other things,"[4] explains the ILO.

For example, human rights groups contend that such exploitation is widespread in Qatar, where migrants constitute 94 percent of the workforce. "Like all migrant workers, domestic workers in Qatar are subject to the highly restrictive *kafala* or sponsorship system, which gives their employer excessive control over them, including the power to deny them the right to leave the country or change jobs,"[5] states Amnesty International (AI). "Like all other foreign workers, they are barred from forming or joining trade unions. In addition, domestic workers cannot challenge their employers if their labour rights are abused, because Qatar's laws specifically prevent them from doing so."[6] Specifically, AI alleges that some domestic migrant workers have been lured to the nation with falsely represented wages or working conditions, forced to work one hundred hours a week with no days off, restricted from leaving the home or using cell phones, verbally or emotionally harassed, and physically or sexually abused.

AI interviewed domestic migrant workers about their experiences in Qatar, some speaking of manipulation, demean-

---

4. Ibid.
5. Amnesty International, *"My Sleep Is My Break": Exploitation of Migrant Domestic Workers in Qatar*, pp. 5–12. London: Amnesty International, 2014. http://www.amnesty.org/en/library/info/MDE22/004/2014/en.
6. Ibid.

ing treatment, and a lack of assistance after victimization. One interviewee claimed that she was explicitly lied to about her income. "The contract I signed in 2009 said I would get US$400 [per month] but when I arrived I was only given 730 riyals [US$200] a month." Another interviewee said that she became trapped in a cycle of beatings by her employer. "She would promise she wouldn't do it again and then after a week would do it again. She pulled me, slapped my face, clutched at my face—she once drew blood from doing this because of her nails." And an interviewee who escaped from an abusive household persisted that her recruitment agency refused to offer any aid. "I called the recruitment agent and they would not help me. I think that this family has a history of problems—I heard that no-one has ever finished a contract with them. The agency told me to do a month's more work and then stopped answering the phone."[7]

However, the abuse of domestic migrant workers is not unique to Qatar. In the United States, reports have surfaced that diplomats have trafficked them into the country through obtaining fraudulent visas for foreign nationals. In 2011, Dominique Strauss-Kahn, former managing director of the International Monetary Fund (IMF), was arrested for sexually assaulting a hotel employee, bringing increased attention to the issue. "Foreign diplomats have been the subject of at least 11 civil lawsuits and one criminal prosecution related to abuse of domestic workers in the last five years, according to a Reuters review of US federal court records,"[8] states Brian Grow, a journalist for Reuters. "The allegations range from slave-like work conditions to rape, and the vast majority of the diplomats in these cases avoided prison terms and financial penalties," he continues. In fact, many diplomats have shielded themselves from prosecution under American laws through

---

7. Ibid.
8. Brian Grow, "Strauss-Kahn Case Raises Issue of Diplomat Abuse in US," Reuters, May 18, 2011. http://mobile.reuters.com/article/idUSTRE74H54320110518?irpc=932.

diplomatic immunity, established by the Vienna Convention on Diplomatic Relations in 1969. "Prosecution of diplomats who abuse their workers is particularly necessary, not only to hopefully improve conditions for a worker but because it may help jar an entire legal regime that has for decades enabled the protection of diplomats who abuse their workers,"[9] writes attorney Sheila Bapat.

The plight of women who travel the globe for domestic work and face abuse and exploitation highlights the major problems of migrant workers from developing countries: unfair wages, appalling working conditions, and human rights violations. But migration for employment has significant impacts on host countries as well, resulting in domestic debates about job competition, income levels, and immigration reform. From policy experts to social activists, the analyses and perspectives compiled in *At Issue: Migrant Workers* explores these topics and more, underlining migrant workers as a part of a complex socioeconomic phenomenon.

9. Sheila Bapat, "Did an Indian Diplomat in the United States Mistreat Her Domestic Worker?," RH Reality Check, January 7, 2014. http://rhrealitycheck.org/article/2014 /01/07/did-an-indian-diplomat-in-the-united-states-mistreat-her-domestic-worker.

1

Migrant Workers Harm Low-Skilled American Workers

Eric A. Ruark and Matthew Graham

Eric A. Ruark is director of research at the Federation for American Immigration Reform (FAIR). Matthew Graham is a policy analyst at the Bipartisan Policy Center and former researcher at FAIR.

Low-skilled illegal immigrants have harmful effects on native workers. The argument that they do not compete with Americans is untrue; most employees of "immigrant" jobs are native workers. Moreover, the claim that illegal immigrants fill shortages in unskilled labor industries is not backed by wage or employment data. In fact, employers underuse unskilled worker programs and turn away teens from employment. And as the least skilled group of the immigrant population, illegal immigrants allow employers to pay lower wages and maintain poor working conditions. Their share of the labor force is also correlated with unemployment among native workers. Granting amnesty to illegal immigrants would increase the surplus of unskilled labor in the economy and encourage illegal immigration.

Immigration policy's effect on the labor force should be carefully considered, but the vast majority of immigrants are not admitted based on education or skill level. In 2009, the U.S. admitted over 1.1 million legal immigrants, just 5.8

percent of whom possessed employment skills in demand in the United States. By contrast, 66.1 percent were based on family preferences, or 73 percent if the relatives of immigrants arriving on employment visas are included. 16.7 percent of admissions were divided among refugees, asylum-seekers and other humanitarian categories, while 4.2 percent of admissions were based on the diversity lottery (which only requires that winners have completed high school). Some family-based immigrants may be highly educated or skilled, but the vast majority of admissions are made without regard for those criteria.

The immigrant population reflects the system's lack of emphasis on skill. Nearly 31 percent of foreign-born residents over the age of 25 are without a high school diploma, compared to just 10 percent of native-born citizens. Immigrants trail natives in rates of college attendance, associate's degrees, and bachelor's degrees, but earn advanced degrees at a slightly higher rate (10.9 percent, compared to 10.4 percent for natives). Illegal immigrants are the least-educated group, with nearly 75 percent having at most a high school education. Overall, 55 percent of the foreign-born population has no education past high school, compared to 42 percent of natives.

The U.S. economy is oversaturated with unskilled labor.

The median immigrant worker has an income of $30,000 per year, trailing native workers by about 18 percent. At $22,500 per year, illegal aliens make even less than their legal counterparts. Though U.S.-born children of legal immigrants are no more likely to be in poverty than those in native households, the children of illegal aliens and foreign-born children of legal immigrants are nearly twice as likely to live in poverty.

Both legal and illegal immigrants lag significantly behind natives in rates of health insurance coverage. Just 14 percent of native adults were uninsured in 2008, compared to 24 percent of legal immigrants and 59 percent of illegal aliens. Children were even more disproportionately uninsured. These low rates of insurance come despite a higher use of Medicaid than native households, 24.4 percent versus 14.7 percent in 2007. Overall, immigrants and their children make up about one-third of the uninsured population.

Immigrants in the Labor Market

A common argument adopted by defenders of illegal immigration is that illegal aliens only take jobs that natives are unwilling or unable to do. In reality, immigrants and natives compete in the same industries, and no job is inherently an "immigrant job." Less than 1 percent of the Census Bureau's 465 civilian job categories have a majority immigrant workforce, meaning that most employees in stereotypically "immigrant occupations" like housekeeping, construction, grounds keeping, janitorial service, and taxi service are actually natives.

The U.S. economy is oversaturated with unskilled labor. In May 2010, the unemployment rate for high school dropouts reached 15 percent, compared to just 4.7 percent among those with a bachelor's degree. If one included workers who are employed part-time for economic reasons or want a job but have given up looking, many more millions of unemployed or underemployed workers are added to that total. Based on this measure, economists Andrew Sum and Ishwar Khatiwada used Current Population Survey data to peg the underutilization rate of high school dropouts at 35 percent, compared to 21 percent for high school graduates, 10 percent for bachelor's recipients, and just 7 percent among advanced degree-earners.

Addressing the Unskilled Labor Surplus

Wage data and occupational patterns also indicate an unskilled labor surplus. The lowest rates of underutilization were found to be in "professional and managerial jobs" like legal, computer, and math-related occupations. Low-skill jobs had by far the highest underutilization rates, with food preparation and service at 24.7 percent, building and grounds cleaning at 24.6 percent, and construction at 32.7 percent. Even before the current economic downturn, indicators revealed a surplus of unskilled labor, as real hourly wages declined by 22 percent among male high school dropouts between 1979 and 2007. For male high school graduates, the drop was 10 percent. Over the same period, real wages for college graduates rose by 23 percent.

The current economic slowdown has reduced labor demand and forced many out of work, making it more important than ever to address the unskilled labor surplus. The labor force participation rate dropped from 63 percent in 2007 to 58.5 percent in June 2010, even while the unemployment rate more than doubled. Job competition has also greatly increased since the onset of the recession. The number of job seekers per job increased from about 1.5 in April 2007 to 5.0 in April 2010, a figure that does not account for underemployed or discouraged workers.

The empirical attempts at supporting the claim that there are not enough Americans to do certain jobs are extremely short-sighted.

Immigration policy and enforcement are two of the most important determinants of America's labor supply, and the U.S. immigration system continues to contribute to the unskilled labor surplus, while the federal government has consistently failed to enforce the laws prohibiting the employment of illegal workers. Between 2000 and 2007, immigration increased the supply of high school dropouts in the labor force by 14.4 percent, compared to just a 2 to 4 percent increase for groups with higher educational attainment. A large share of the increase in unskilled labor was caused by illegal entry—over the same period, an estimated four million illegal immigrants took up residence in the U.S., about two million of whom had no diploma and another million of whom had no education past high school.

The large influx of unskilled, sometimes desperate workers has allowed employers to offer low wages and deplorable conditions. Special interests have successfully promoted the myth that Americans refuse to do some jobs, but in truth, immigrants and natives work alongside one another in all low-skill occupations. Reducing low-skill immigration, especially illegal immigration, would tighten the labor market and force employers to increase wages and improve working conditions.

Extremely Short-Sighted Findings

The empirical attempts at supporting the claim that there are not enough Americans to do certain jobs are extremely short-sighted. Some reports, including the Immigration Policy Center's "Untying the Knot" series, have taken any observable demographic difference between immigrants and natives to imply that they do not compete for jobs. In one case, the authors write that, "[t]here were 390,000 unemployed natives without a high-school diploma who had no occupation, compared to zero employed recent immigrants without a high-school diploma." In other words, the authors limit the sample to people who *report having no occupation*, then claim that because no immigrants who *do* have an occupation have the same education level as some unemployed natives, there is no competition between immigrants and natives. This is not evidence of anything.

Every "finding" made in the "Untying the Knot" series is consistent with an assumed lack of immigrant-native competition. The authors attempt to prove that immigrants and natives of different skill levels live in different parts of the country by making observations like, "the largest share (26.9

percent) of all employed recent immigrants without a high school diploma lived in the Pacific states . . . [b]ut the largest share (18.9 percent) of unemployed natives without a high-school diploma lived in the East North Central states." These percentages gloss over the reality that there are millions of low-skill natives in Pacific states and millions of immigrants in East North Central states. The authors attempt to use slight differences in regional demographics to mask the fact that there are immigrants and natives competing within the same skill levels and occupations in every part of the country.

It would make no sense to grant permanent legal status and full job market access to millions of unskilled illegal alien workers at the expense of [the unemployed] 12.9 million natives.

Just as importantly, the study's attempt to use regional differences to disprove immigrant-native competition is seriously flawed. Downward wage pressure and job displacement occurs nationally, rendering local differences less significant. For example, the shift toward illegal labor in the meatpacking industry moved production from urban to rural areas and applied cost-cutting pressure to meat producers everywhere. Natives in one part of the country lost jobs to illegal immigrants in another part. The claims in "Untying the Knot" are meaningless and misleading, and the premise of the claims out of touch with the realities of the U.S. labor market. Nonetheless, pro-amnesty groups apparently found the report's baseless conclusions to be quite useful—the Immigration Policy Center, an offshoot of the American Immigration Lawyers Association, touted the report as its second most utilized resource in 2009.

Employers Are Interested Parties

Others looking to justify a need for unskilled labor treat employers as if they were not interested parties. Employers often claim shortages of unskilled labor to justify their need for a constant supply of migrant workers, whether legal or illegal. These claims are not backed by wage patterns or employment data. In fact, employers do not take full advantage of existing unskilled worker programs. The H-2A visa for temporary agricultural workers is uncapped, meaning that employers could legally bring in as many seasonal laborers as they need through the H-2B visa program, the demand for which was so low in 2009 that USCIS extended the application deadline and ultimately left about 10,000 visas unclaimed at the end of the year. Claims that farmers would be unable to harvest their crops without illegal immigrants are pure fiction. Instead, they could use legal immigrants or natives.

In addition to the practice of hiring illegal aliens rather than using legal guest worker programs, employers have turned away from hiring teens. The steep decline in teen employment since the 1980s, both year-round and during the summer, is unprecedented for any demographic group in American history. Teen summer employment hit a 60-year low in 2008, with just 32.7 percent of teens holding a summer job. Over 3.4 million teens were either unemployed, underemployed, or part of the labor force reserve that summer. The households who have suffered most are the ones that would benefit most from another income-earner—low-income teens were nearly twice as likely to be underutilized as high-income teens.

Overall, there is a massive pool of unskilled natives that needs work. In May 2010, 7.1 million natives with a high school diploma or less were unemployed, another 3.1 million were not considered part of the labor force but reported wanting a job, and 2.7 million more were working part-time for an economic reason. It would make no sense to grant permanent legal status and full job market access to millions of unskilled illegal alien workers at the expense of these 12.9 million natives, not to mention the millions more whose wages have been undercut by low-skill immigration. Politicians should not succumb to corporate America's addiction to ever-growing quantities of unskilled immigrant labor.

Impact on Poor Americans

Regardless of their views about the overall economic effect of immigration, almost all economists agree that poor native workers bear the brunt of its negative consequences. Foreign-born workers compete with natives on all skill levels, but because immigrants to the U.S. are disproportionately unskilled, they are especially likely to undercut the wages of low-skill natives. An analysis of America's 25 largest metropolitan areas showed that in high-skill industry groups like health professionals, technicians, administrative workers, and educators, immigrant earnings were usually within 10 percent of native wages; however, in unskilled groups like construction, machine operators, drivers, and farming, foreign-born workers consistently earned at least 10 percent less than their peers. Immigrant-native competition is an important concern in high-skill jobs, but is much more acute in low-skill industries.

If legal and illegal immigration continue to add to the overabundance of unskilled workers, the consequences for poor natives will continue to grow.

Illegal aliens are the least skilled subset of the immigrant population, and therefore the most likely to undercut the wages and working conditions of low-skilled natives. Among seventeen industry categories named by the Pew Research Center as having the highest proportions of illegal aliens, data from the Current Population Survey reveal that noncitizens earned lower wages than natives in all but one of them. Data for noncitizens, which includes legal and illegal immigrants as well as temporary laborers, differ from data on illegal aliens because the latter tend to have lower wages and fewer skills. However, data on noncitizens are a much better fit for illegal aliens than using the foreign born population as a whole. In construction, noncitizens earned less than two-thirds of natives' wage salaries, and in the two agricultural categories, they earned less than half. Wage and salary differences demonstrate how illegal and unskilled immigrants place downward pressure on wages by providing an incentive for employers to choose them over natives. The opportunity to exploit workers is the reason big business clamors for more immigrant labor.

Most wage-effect studies do not analyze illegal immigrants as a separate group because most demographic data is not differentiated on that basis. However, what evidence does exist indicates that they constitute a major drag on unskilled wages. In 2010, Raúl Hinojosa-Ojeda of the Center for American Progress estimated that unskilled workers would on average make about $400 more per year if the illegal immigrant population were reduced by 4 million, or approximately one-third. In Georgia, where the illegal immigrant share of the labor force went from about 4 percent to 7 percent from 2000 to 2007, a study by the Federal Reserve found that the illegal labor caused a 2.5 percent wage drop overall and an 11 percent drop in construction wages over the period. This analysis used a confidential state employer database that helped identify Social Security mismatches, making it one of the most sophisticated estimates available.

Other estimates focus on the entire immigrant population, whose education is comparable to natives at the high end but overwhelmingly unskilled at the other end of the distribution. The National Research Council's landmark 1997 study estimated that high school dropouts earn 5 percent less per year due to immigration, which totaled $13 billion in wage losses at a time when the illegal alien population stood at less than half its present number. Harvard University's George Borjas concluded that immigration reduced wages for the poorest 10 percent of Americans by about 7-4 percent between 1980 and 2000 with even larger effects for workers with less than 20 years of experience. Other economists who have found that immigration depresses low-skilled wages include the Cato Institute's Daniel Griswold. If legal and illegal immigration continue to add to the overabundance of unskilled workers, the consequences for poor natives will continue to grow.

The Strong Link Between Low-Skill Immigrant Labor and Native Unemployment

A strong link exists between low-skill immigrant labor and native unemployment. Steve Camarota of the Center for Immigration Studies found a correlation of 0.9 between low-skill immigrants' share of an occupation and the native unemployment rate in that occupation; the correlation between the illegal immigrant share of an occupation and native unemployment was also high at 0.91 (the highest possible correlation is 1). Translated from statistical terminology, these numbers show that illegal and low-skill immigration go hand-in-hand with a rise in native unemployment. The share of illegal and low-skill immigrants in a job category explains about 80 percent of the variance in native unemployment between different occupations.

Any large-scale immigration reform must address the impact of both legal and illegal immigration on the unskilled labor surplus. Congress could easily mandate cost effective employer-based measures such as E-Verify that would deter illegal immigration and encourage voluntary emigration due to decreasing employment opportunities for illegal workers. Illegal aliens are rational people. Most come seeking a job and generally will leave when they cannot find one. Border security and deportation are key elements of immigration enforcement, but effectively denying employment opportunities is the most efficient and effective way to keep illegal immigrants out of the country.

If employers were required to hire legal workers and pay fair market wages, the vast pool of native unskilled labor would fill these positions. On the other hand, if Congress were to grant amnesty to illegal immigrants, it would perpetuate the oversupply of unskilled workers. Based on past history, the response to a mass amnesty would be high rates of future illegal immigration as the expectation that coming to the U.S. illegally would be rewarded is reinforced.

2

Migrant Workers Do Not Harm Low-Skilled American Workers

Michael A. Clemens

Michael A. Clemens is senior fellow at the Center for Global Development.

Labor economics research robustly finds that immigration does not harm low-skill American workers. First, migrant workers and native workers do not compete for the same jobs; the statistics demonstrate that there are not enough Americans to fill the fastest-growing occupations, which do not require a high school education. Furthermore, the indirect impacts of low-skill migrant labor create other positions for low-skill workers. This includes migrants' consumption of labor across all skill groups, their specialization in skills that differ from low-skill native workers, and employment in agriculture and industries that would shut down without migrant labor. The effects of immigration boost the nation's economic productivity, creating jobs for Americans and migrants.

The heated debate over immigration reform continues in Washington. Much of the heat comes from one claim: immigration hurts low-skill US workers.

The idea is that immigration causes overall economic harm to low-skill US workers, because many immigrants are low-

Michael A. Clemens, "The Case That Immigrant Labor Doesn't Hurt Low-skill U.S. Workers," alternet.org, June 4, 2013. Copyright © 2013 Michael A. Clemens. All rights reserved. Reproduced with permission.

skill themselves and compete for the same jobs. This is a reasonable belief if all one has to go on is the kind of day-to-day experiences that everyone has—such as applying for jobs and competing with other applicants.

It is also wrong.

Many of the world's best labor economists have spent the last quarter century exhaustively looking all over the world for negative effects of immigration on low-skill workers. They cannot find such effects. This is one of the most robust findings in the labor economics research literature.

Two Main Approaches

These economists take two main approaches. The first is to look for sudden, large increases in immigration to a particular area, and track what happens to native workers in that area. These include massive inflows of Cubans to Miami in 1980, Algerians to France in 1962, Russians to Israel in the early 1990s, all immigrants to different regions of Germany in the 1980s and to regions of the United Kingdom in the 80s and 90s, and former Yugoslavians to the rest of Europe. Not one detects substantial effects of immigration on wages or employment.

The problem is not that Americans entering the labor force aren't willing to take certain jobs. It's that there aren't enough Americans to do them.

In the second approach, economists chop up the data differently. They divide workers in the migrant-destination country not into different geographic regions but into different groups of broadly similar people—for example, 25–29 year-old males with a high school degree, 30–34 year-old females with a college degree, and so on. They then watch what happens to wages and employment among native workers in each group, across the whole country, upon the arrival of immigrants with those characteristics. With this method, the leading-edge research is by Gianmarco Ottaviano and Giovanni Peri. In a paper published last year [in 2012], they show that total, cumulative immigration to the United States between 1990 and 2006 had almost no net effect on the wages of American workers—including those with no high school degree.

How did our common-sense intuition get this crucial fact so wrong? Our best understanding now is that two broad forces yield this counterintuitive result. For the low-skill jobs that exist, there is extremely little competition between native workers and immigrant workers. And the indirect economic effects of low-skill immigrants' work are the reason that many low-skill jobs exist in the first place, including the ones filled by native workers.

Not Competing with U.S. Workers

First, the vast majority of low-skill immigrants are not competing with any U.S. worker at all. The problem is not that Americans entering the labor force aren't willing to take certain jobs. It's that there aren't enough Americans to do them.

In the next decade most of the fastest-growing occupations will be jobs that require less than high school education. The US Bureau of Labor Statistic projects that between 2010 and 2020 there will be 3.6 million new, additional jobs in the US economy in home health care, basic childcare, and food service, and other low-skill industries. That is, the Census Bureau reports, more than double the total American workers age 25–54 who will enter the labor force in the same period: 1.7 million.

This point bears repeating: even if every single American entering the labor force in the next decade dropped out of high school and college to do low-skill work, they wouldn't be able to fill half the labor positions America needs in these areas. And of course that isn't going to happen: In that period roughly 30 percent of Americans entering the labor force will have high school only, and under 10 percent will have less than high school. That means we can reasonably expect somewhere around 5–15 percent of these very low-skill jobs to be filled by American workers. For the rest, no American will be competing with immigrants.

Indirectly Creating New Jobs

Second, low-skill immigrant labor has numerous economic effects that end up, indirectly, creating new jobs for low-skill workers—including American workers. These effects are difficult to observe precisely because they are indirect.

Workers outside immigrants' skill groups depend on the labor of immigrants to make occupation and education decisions that raise their own productivity.

Economists have identified these and other indirect ways that low-skill immigrant workers create jobs for other low-skill workers:

- Low-skill immigrants are not just sellers of their own labor; they spend money, meaning that they are consumers of other people's labor—across all skill groups.

- Very low-skill immigrant workers tend to specialize in different tasks than moderately low-skill American workers. For example, on many American farms, native workers with some high school education often perform very different jobs than immigrant workers with no high school education.

- Low-skill immigrant workers make other workers' paychecks go further by making basic services like restaurant food and landscaping more affordable and thus driving up the demand for low-skill workers.

- Low-skill immigrants cause more high-skill U.S. women to enter the labor force, by making childcare and elder-care more affordable.

- Low-skill immigrants encourage U.S. workers to stay in high school, so that they don't have to compete with immigrants for low-skill jobs.

- Low-skill immigrants also keep entire U.S. industries alive: many parts of U.S. agriculture would have had to close up shop years ago if not for low-skill workers who pick the crop, and that would mean the loss of all U.S. jobs in those sectors.

All of these forces tend to raise the productivity of the whole economy, generating jobs en masse, including low-skill jobs for both American and immigrant workers. It is understandably hard for people to believe in effects like these, because they are indirect and hard to discern. How, a reasonable person might ask, can a Guatemalan nanny changing diapers have broad effects on US economic productivity? You have to think for a moment about what you don't see: the economic activity that the child's mother is thereby freed up to perform, and how the ripple effects of that mother's work end up bolstering whole industries and creating new jobs.

The Backbone of the American Economy

These indirect effects are the key to understanding the difference between the repeated, robust findings of this literature and the better-known research of George Borjas at the Harvard Kennedy School. In a paper published ten years ago, Borjas measured the effect of additional immigrant labor on native workers when many of these indirect effects do not occur. For example, the Borjas paper assumes that low-skill natives and lower-skill immigrants do not complement each other by specializing in different tasks, and it assumes that lower-skill workers do not raise the productivity of higher-skill workers (as when a low-skill immigrant nanny allows a high-skill US woman to enter the labor force). If what you want to do is measure the pure, idealized relationship between the amount of labor and its price, the ways that other workers react to and accommodate inflows of immigrant labor are a distraction. If instead what you want to do is measure what really happens in an economy when immigrants enter it, it is critical to account for the ways that other workers react and accommodate the flows. Workers within immigrants' skill groups specialize in different tasks to avoid competing with them, and workers outside immigrants' skill groups depend on the labor of immigrants to make occupation and education decisions that raise their own productivity. Borjas' work removes these effects, Ottaviano and Peri's work includes them. Both are high-quality economic research, but only the more recent work of Ottaviano and Peri addresses the full effects of immigrant workers on US workers.

The closest thing that science has to "laws" are findings that pass empirical tests again and again, in all kinds of settings. Immigrant labor is still an active area of research, but the absence of substantial negative labor-market impacts of immigrants on native workers may be one such broad, robust finding. This discovery will certainly take a long time to enter the public consciousness, if it ever does. In the meantime, public discourse will likely go on assuming that low-skill immigrants are somehow economically harmful. In fact, low-skill workers are now and have always been the backbone of the American economy. A substantial majority of the ancestors of today's Americans arrived here as low-skill immigrants, not PhDs. Low-skill immigrants are not "cheap labor": they typically earn vastly more in the United States than they could at home, and thanks to migration their labor is receiving proper compensation for the first time in their lives. Low-skill immigrants are foundational to the U.S. economy: every job, from janitors to biochemists, depends on a legion of low-skill workers that made that job possible. Throughout history that economic contribution has been contested and ignored. Whether recent discoveries in social science can alter that pattern remains to be seen.

3

Migrant Workers and American Workers Face the Same Problems

Saket Soni

Saket Soni is the executive director of the National Guestworker Alliance and the New Orleans Workers' Center for Racial Justice.

More and more American workers are being treated as disposable commodities, facing the instabilities and injustices that have long affected migrant workers. Currently, one-third of employment positions in the United States are contingent—part-time or contracted—leaving more families without health insurance, pensions, and other benefits of full-time employment. Despite working harder and longer, their wages have stagnated, and larger corporations now dominate employment and job creation, driving down compensation and controlling working conditions. As long as migrant workers and immigration reform are viewed as threats, the United States will remain unprepared to address the shift toward a low-wage national economy.

When members of Congress come back from recess, they could put our nation's 11.7 million undocumented immigrant workers on a path to citizenship. But if they refuse to, as they did in 2013, they'll be pushing US workers further down the path to becoming like low-wage immigrant workers. After all, our economy is already headed in exactly that direction.

Move over, farmers, factory workers and technology "creatives"—the emblematic American workers are now low-wage immigrant day laborers and guest workers. More and more, Americans are trapped in the uncertainty and injustice that immigrant workers know all too well, whether they're here on temporary work visas cleaning luxury condos or undocumented and scrambling for daily construction jobs. Increasingly, from an economic standpoint, office parks and store aisles in America are coming to resemble the street corners where day laborers gather and the labor camps where guest workers are trapped. We can either continue to pretend that low-wage immigrant workers are on the fringes of our economy—that their problems are theirs alone—or we can face the fact that their conditions are what we're all moving toward, and what millions of US-born workers already face.

The United States, which presents itself as a global beacon of opportunity and prosperity, is quickly becoming a low-wage nation.

More Without Employment Certainty

Immigrant workers have long experienced vulnerability and instability, and have long been treated as disposable by their employers. Today, roughly one-third of American jobs are part-time, contract or otherwise "contingent." And the number of contingent workers in the United States is expected to grow by more than one-third over the next four years. That means more and more families are without the benefits of full-time work, such as health insurance, pensions or 401(k)s. And more of us are without the employment certainty that leads to economic stability at home—and to the consumer spending that drives the economy.

In addition, while we are working longer and harder, wages are stagnant. Between 2000 and 2011, the US economy grew by more than 18 percent, while the median income for working families declined by 12.4 percent. Once upon a time, workers shared the economic prosperity of their employers: until 1975, wages accounted for more than 50 percent of America's GDP. But by 2013, wages had fallen to a record low of just 43.5 percent of GDP. Overall compensation, which factors in healthcare and other benefits, has also hit bottom. Immigrants know where this downward spiral leads—just ask the Jamaican guest workers who cleaned luxury beach condos in Florida last summer and came away with paychecks for zero dollars and zero cents.

And like countless immigrant workers, more and more American workers are trapped in supply and subcontracting chains for big and powerful employers. From the late 1970s until the 2008 recession, small businesses were the prime generator of jobs in America, creating roughly 60 percent of all employment. That percentage has been swiftly declining ever since. The percentage of business loans going to small start-ups has also declined. And yet small businesses generally pay higher wages than large corporations, and a significantly higher percentage of every dollar spent at a small business stays in the community and further boosts the local economy, as opposed to dollars fleeing to often distant corporate headquarters. But when large employers dominate an industry or town, they have unchecked power to drive down wages and working conditional—or, in some cases, to try to avoid paying any wages at all. In 2012, Walmart agreed to pay $4.83 million in overdue back wages to more than 4,500 workers. And conditions don't get much worse than those of guest workers in the Walmart supply chain who exposed captive labor at a company called CJ's Seafood that same year, where a supervisor threatened to beat workers with a shovel to make them work faster.

A Low-Wage Nation

The United States, which presents itself as a global beacon of opportunity and prosperity, is quickly becoming a low-wage nation. America's immigrant workers are the proverbial canaries in the coal mine—and the coal mine extends from construction sites to supermarkets to Silicon Valley.

We as a nation will be ill equipped to address this profound shift as long as we cling to the divisive vision of an "us and them" economy. Some Americans resist immigration reform because they sense the transformation in the nature of work in our country and make immigrants the target of their justified anxiety. In fact, all US workers—immigrants and US-born, low-wage and higher-wage, temporary and full-time—are increasingly in the same boat. The sooner we realize that we all face the predicament of immigrant workers, the sooner we can work together to solve structural inequality in our economy instead of fighting over the crumbs.

4

Migrant Workers and America's Harvest of Shame

Ralph Nader

Ralph Nader is a consumer advocate, attorney, and author of numerous books, including The Seventeen Solutions: Bold Ideas for Our American Future.

The plight of migrant farmworkers has not changed for more than fifty years. Other than the very few working under a union contract, those who toil in backbreaking conditions in the fields are perversely underpaid and underprotected while agribusiness reaps the profits. Migrant farmworkers are excluded from the Fair Labor Standards Act and exposed to dangerous levels of pesticides due to the outmoded Worker Protection Standards. In addition, the federal minimum wage does not apply to them; undocumented farmworkers are paid the least. Still, Congress has done little to raise awareness of their plight, and federal labor laws must be amended to protect their wages and well-being, not the interests of agribusiness.

The great reporter Edward R. Murrow titled his 1960 CBS documentary *Harvest of Shame* on the merciless exploitation of the migrant farmworkers by the large growers and their local government allies. Over fifty years later, it is still the harvest of shame for nearly two million migrant farmworkers who follow the seasons and the crops to harvest our fruits and vegetables.

As a student I went through migrant farmworker camps and fields and wrote about the abysmally low pay, toxic, unsafe working conditions, contaminated water, housing hovels and the complete absence of any legal rights.

It is a perversely inverted society when the people who do the backbreaking work to harvest one of the necessities of life are underpaid, underinsured, under-protected and under-respected while the Chicago commodity brokers—where the white collar gamblers sit in air-conditioned spaces and speculate on futures in foodstuffs' prices—are quite well off, to put it modestly.

It probably won't surprise you that the grapes, peaches, watermelons, strawberries, apricots and lettuce that you're eating this week are brought to you from the fields by the descendants of the early migrant workers. Their plight is not that much better, except for the very few working under a real union contract.

Perhaps as many as half a million children, some as young as seven years old, are out in the fields and orchards working nine to ten hour days under brutal conditions.

Start with the exclusion of farmworkers from the Fair Labor Standards Act. Then go to the EPA's Worker Protection Standard (WPS), which is aimed at protecting farmworkers and their families from pesticides but is outdated, weak and poorly enforced.

Continue on to the unyielding local power of growers and their campaign-cash indentured local, state and congressional lawmakers. The recent shocking description of the tomato workers in central Florida in Chris Hedges and Joe Sacco's book *Days of Destruction, Days of Revolt*, shows how close defenseless migrant workers can come to involuntary servitude.

In a recent television interview, featuring Baldemar Velasquez—a vigorous farm worker organizer—Bill Moyers summarized the period since *Harvest of Shame*: "Believe it or not, more than fifty years later, the life of a migrant laborer is still an ordeal. And not just for adults. Perhaps as many as half a million children, some as young as seven years old, are out in the fields and orchards working nine to ten hour days under brutal conditions."

Among the conditions Moyers was referring to are the daily exposures to pesticides, fertilizers and the resulting chemical-related injuries and sicknesses. Far more of these pesticides end up in the workers' bodies than are found in our food. President of Farmworker Justice, Bruce Goldstein writes: "Short-term effects include stinging eyes, rashes, blisters, blindness, nausea, dizziness, headache, coma and even death. Pesticides also cause infertility, neurological disorders and cancer."

In a recent letter appeal by the United Farm Workers (UFW), the beleaguered small union representing farmworkers, these ailments were connected to real workers by name. Focusing on the large grape grower—Giumarra Vineyards of California—the UFW describes one tragedy of many: "After ten hours laboring under a blazing July sun, 53-year-old Giumarra grape picker Asuncion Valdivia became weak, dizzy and nauseated. He couldn't talk. He lay down in the field. The temperature was 102 degrees.

"Asuncion's 21-year-old son, Luis, and another worker rushed to his aid. Someone called 911. But a Giumarra foreman cancelled the paramedics. He told Luis to drive his father home. They reached the emergency room in Bakersfield too late. Asuncion died on the car seat next to his son."

For backbreaking work, kneeling 48 hours a week on crippled joints, 29-year-old Alejandro Ruiz and other farmworkers are not making much to live on. The federal minimum wage of $7.25 an hour does not apply to farmworkers.

Workers without documents are often paid less than those with documents. In most cases, they are too frightened to consider objecting.

It is so deplorable how little the members of Congress from these farm districts have done to improve the plight of migrant farm workers. Members of Congress could be raising the visibility of deplorable working conditions faced by farmworkers and allying themselves with urban district Representatives concerned about food safety. This partnership could raise awareness of the safety of the food supply, the careless use of agricultural chemicals, and press the EPA to issue a strong WPS that emphasizes training, disclosure of chemical usage, safety precautions prior to spraying and buffer zones.

Is there a more compelling case for union organizing than the farm workers who sweat for agri-business? Federal labor laws need to be amended to improve national standards for farmworkers and eliminate existing state fair wage and health barriers. California has the strongest law, passed under the first gubernatorial term of Jerry Brown in 1975. Even this law needs to be strengthened to overcome the ways it has been gamed by agri-business interests.

Next time you eat fruits or vegetables, pause a moment to imagine what the workers who harvested them had to endure and talk up their plight with your friends and co-workers. Remember, every reform starts with human conversations and awareness.

5

Migrant Child Farmworkers Are Exploited

Arturo Conde

Arturo Conde is a journalist, editor of About.com en Español, and the former director of the North American Congress on Latin America (NACLA).

Even in wealthy countries like the United States, migrant child farmworkers pay the human cost of what we eat. To support their impoverished families, children ages twelve and under work up to fourteen hours a day, seven days a week, in harsh conditions and without the guarantee of a minimum wage. Financially dependent on the harvest season, they are unable to complete their education and much more likely to drop out of school, which traps them in a cycle of poverty. Despite migrant child farmworkers' hard work and sacrifices, they are discriminated against and treated as indentured servants. Though some have grown up and become successful, very few are able to break free of the cycle of poverty and despair.

U. Roberto Romano's 2011 documentary *The Harvest (La Cosecha)* reminds us of the human cost of what we eat. "In some countries, children work 14 hours a day, seven days a week," he explains in the film. "In some countries, children 12 and younger pick crops. The United States of America is one of those countries."

Romano's documentary compels viewers to come to terms with the uncomfortable reality that in a country like the United States, where there is so much wealth, modern cities, and plentiful resources, many people still endure inequality and poverty.

The Harvest begins with the testimonies of three children. "I pick strawberries, cherries, pickles, and oranges," says a young girl. "I just wanted to vomit 'cause [of] the sun and smell of tomatoes," says a teenage boy. "The cotton plants when I was 10 looked like skyscrapers," says another teenage girl.

We soon find out that the voices of the underage workers belong to the child migrant farmers Zulema López, 12; Victor Huapilla, 16; and Perla Sánchez, 14. The documentary profiles the lives of these children and their families on the fields, as they migrate from harvest to harvest across the United States.

López typically wakes up at 4:30 a.m. on a workday, picks crops nearly 12 hours a day, and earns only $64 per week.

Trapped in a Cycle of Poverty

Romano's film underlines the fact that every year, over 400,000 children pick the food that we eat in 48 states. These children often come from multiple generations of migrant farming, and their families are unable to break away from the cycle of poverty.

"Why don't we have any money?" asks Sánchez. "Because we can't finish school."

Many migrant children can't finish high school because their financial dependence on the harvest season forces them to leave early, hindering their ability to study and get good grades. López's mom explains how she was similarly trapped by this cycle and hopes that her children can aspire to a better life.

"When I was little, my dreams were to finish school, go to college," she says. "Now that I couldn't do that, I want my kids to be something in their lives. I tell them, you know, I don't want to see you guys like me."

For many migrant families, education is the only way out. But for someone like López, who started picking crops at seven years old, dedicating herself to school is unrealistic when she is also laboring long hours on the fields.

"I feel like I'm left behind," López says, comparing herself to other students. "I don't even think I am going to make it to high school or anything."

According to Romano, migrant children drop out of school at four times the national rate. When the viewer sees that López typically wakes up at 4:30 a.m. on a workday, picks crops nearly 12 hours a day, and earns only $64 per week, it becomes clear that her difficult circumstances outweigh the prospects of getting a good education. Yet in spite of her hardships and ongoing insecurities, López is grateful that she is still with her family.

"Why is it suffering if I am not the only one who has to move?" she asks.

Faces of the U.S. Working Class

Many child farmers rely on their families as a source of stability.

"My inspiration is my family," says Huapilla. He labors long hours on the fields so that his family can avoid any further hardships.

"I worked to help my parents when I saw they couldn't manage," he says. "Even though they never ask for it, I want to do it anyway."

Huapilla gets paid $1 for every bucket of tomatoes that he collects. Each bucket weighs 25 pounds, and on a good day, he can carry over 1,500 pounds. Migrant children have no guaranteed minimum wage or overtime, and by the end of one shift, Huapilla's hands are often blistered and rough. Soap alone won't remove the thick layer of tomato juice and dirt that sticks to his skin, so he has to use bleach to scrub himself clean.

This sense of commitment compels the viewer to see Huapilla and the other children as the faces of the U.S. working class. Their plight personifies the hardships and sacrifices that most working-class families have to endure to remain together. During one rare moment in the film, we see Huapilla in school and get the sense that while his condition as a migrant worker is tragic, it can also be heroic in the context of his family. Huapilla's teacher describes how "ordinary people like us" could become heroes in small ways. And according to this definition of heroism, every fruit or vegetable that Huapilla picks is a courageous step that helps his family move ahead.

Sánchez is put down constantly by people who blame her condition as a migrant, and her family's poverty, on stupidity.

Facing Discrimination

Other migrant children like Sánchez, however, face discrimination in spite of their sacrifices.

"Just because you're brown, they think you are from Mexico," she says. "They tell you to go back to Mexico, go back to where you came from, without them knowing that I was born here. Where am I supposed to go?"

Sánchez is put down constantly by people who blame her condition as a migrant, and her family's poverty, on stupidity. But she defends herself on camera by reminding the viewer that being a migrant is not about having made bad choices. These migrants simply don't have time to be anything else.

"Time doesn't stop because you are doing this [picking crops]," says Sánchez. "Time doesn't stop because you are migrating. Time goes, and if it goes, it goes faster."

Yet no matter how antithetical these children's lives are to notions of the American dream, their endurance, which stems more from stubbornness than resilience, makes them hopeful.

"I have a dream to become a lawyer," says Sánchez. "I have a dream to help other people stop being migrants. I have so many dreams to help other people just like me."

Romano's film ends on an upbeat note, paying tribute to role models—an astronaut, the director of a brain surgery program, and a distinguished academic, among others—who had been migrant children and were able to escape the cycle of poverty. But for many viewers, the lives of these role models are clearly an exception.

Migrants will continue to live like indentured servants as long as U.S. society treats them with indifference. By empathizing with these people, we will understand that they are not too different from our own families—ordinary men, women, and children who are on a quest for a better life.

6

Some Working Conditions of Migrant Farmworkers Have Improved

Barry Estabrook

Barry Estabrook is the author of Tomatoland: How Modern Industrial Agriculture Destroyed Our Most Alluring Fruit *and a
former contributing editor at* Gourmet *magazine.*

*The Fair Food Agreement of 2011 has improved the working
conditions of some migrant farmworkers. At a tomato farm in
Florida, its terms resulted in positive changes. Punch clocks were
introduced for pickers to keep track of their hours worked and
ensure payment of the correct wages. Growers promised pickers a
penny more per pound if paid by buyers, which can increase a
daily wage from $50 to $80 a day. Furthermore, growers established health and safety rules—including shade and sufficient
breaks for pickers and policies against sexual harassment—along
with a system for filing complaints without fear of termination.
Still, the majority of national supermarkets have not signed the
Fair Food Agreement, leaving many pickers without the extra
wages and whole sectors of the workforce vulnerable to exploitation.*

On a crisp, sunny spring morning in 2011, I did something that could well have gotten me arrested only a few
months earlier. I rode south of Immokalee in a road-weary

Barry Estabrook, "New World, Old Challenges," *Tomatoland: How Modern Industrial Agriculture Destroyed Our Most Alluring Fruit.* Kansas City: Andrews McMeel Publishing,
2012, pp. 189–194. Copyright © 2012 Andrews McMeel Publishing. All rights reserved.
Reproduced with permission.

Toyota with Lucas Benitez and three other members of the Coalition of Immokalee Workers (CIW). We slowed as we arrived at the security gates in front of a packing plant owned by Pacific Tomato Growers, a major fruit and vegetable producer with farms in Florida, Georgia, Virginia, California, and Mexico. Consumers know the company through its brand names Sunripe and Suncoast. During the course of nearly two decades of struggling to improve working conditions and end abuses in Florida's fields, the CIW had come calling on the Pacific facility numerous times to present its demands, each time to be met with locked gates. "One time, there were sheriff's officers with guns," said Benitez. On this occasion, officials at the company did not know that I was accompanying the CIW members. I scrunched in my seat, trying to look inconspicuous.

I needn't have bothered; the watchman gave a smile and a nod as the car cruised past the guardhouse. In a parking lot beyond it, we encountered a gathering that would have been as unlikely at an earlier time in the Florida tomato patch as the CIW's visit to the packing plant. A school bus had stopped in front of a building that resembled a carport. Its wooden trusses and timbers were fresh, blond colored, and had obviously been removed only recently from a lumber warehouse, nailed together, and exposed to the sun and humidity of Florida. A bank of solar panels rested in its roof. Members of a harvest crew filed from the bus and stood in front of what looked like a bank of ATMs. Actually, the machines were yet another novelty in the Florida tomato industry: punch clocks that would keep track of every minute the pickers worked and guarantee that they received the right wages.

Once on the clock and being paid for their time, the workers—Hispanic and clad in jeans, T-shirts, and either baseball caps or straw cowboy hats—ambled in groups of two or three toward a modular building with a sign near the door that read TRAINING. About fifty pickers had already gathered on folding chairs inside when the CIW delegation entered and began preparing to lead a class designed to educate the field crew about their rights and responsibilities under a new program called the Fair Food Agreement. I took a seat in the far back corner.

Shaking hands and signing a feel-good agreement in the shade of a tree is one thing. Making that agreement work in gritty, remote Florida tomato fields is an entirely different matter.

The Terms of the Fair Food Agreement

The Fair Food Agreement had been signed only five months earlier on a folding table under a tree in back of the CIW headquarters by Reggie Brown, the executive vice president of the Florida Tomato Growers Exchange, the agricultural cooperative whose members grow virtually all of Florida's tomatoes. According to the terms of the Fair Food Agreement, the growers promised to pass along an extra penny a pound to pickers if—and this is a crucial "if"—the end buyer of the tomatoes had also signed the agreement and agreed to pay the penny. It doesn't sound like much, but for an average worker it's the difference between making $50 and $80 a day—between abject poverty and a living, albeit hardscrabble, wage. More important, the agreement also requires that companies use time clocks like the one the workers were punching that morning to make sure that they earn at least the $7.25 minimum hourly wage to which they are entitled. A system has been put in place so workers can complain about injustices without fear of being fired. Health and safety rules were established, requiring farms to provide shade for workers; guaranteeing them a sufficient number of work breaks, including time for lunch; and introducing a stern policy to combat sexual harassment—all too common in the fields. These are all rights that the average American takes for granted, but they had never applied to tomato workers. It was as if a Dickensian workhouse had overnight adopted the labor practices of a state-of-the-art auto plant.

Rolling Out the Policies

But shaking hands and signing a feel-good agreement in the shade of a tree is one thing. Making that agreement work in gritty, remote Florida tomato fields is an entirely different matter. The coalition members and the executives of the companies represented by Reggie Brown, who had previously not even been on speaking terms, suddenly found themselves in a position where they would have to communicate and work cooperatively to transform the fine words of the Fair Food Agreement into tangible deeds. Together, the growers' and workers' representatives decided that the 2010-to-2011 growing season would be a period of transition. Pacific and Six L's (since renamed Lipman), the two large tomato growers on whose fields pickers who worked under the infamous Navarrete slavery gang had once toiled, took the lead. Almost immediately after the agreement was signed, they began to work with the coalition to find practical ways of introducing a new Code of Conduct to the Florida tomato industry on a limited basis. Once they had worked through practical kinks at their two companies, the policies would be rolled out during the 2011-to-2012 growing season to every member of the exchange that had signed the Fair Food Agreement—meaning that virtually every tomato picker in Florida would benefit from higher wages; more stringent safety standards; a clear system for lodging complaints; and protection from sexual harassment, enslavement, and other abuses. To make sure that they understand their rights and responsibilities under the new system, all fifty thousand workers who pick tomatoes in Florida each year will attend classes like the one I joined last spring. They also will be required to watch a video that illustrates those rights in simple, clearly comprehensible images and language.

The definition of what constituted a full bucket had long been a source of tension, disputes, and occasionally fistfights in the fields.

Inside the education building, the CIW's Benitez was greeted by Angel Garcia, the human-resources manager of Pacific. Physically, the two men were a study in contrasts: Benitez, short and compact, with a wrestler's build and an intense demeanor; Garcia, large, bearlike, and soft spoken. In the 1990s, Benitez was just another Mexican teenager loading tomatoes into a bucket in the fields spreading out to the horizon behind the packing house. Today, he and Garcia would address members of a crew much like the one to which Benitez once belonged.

Over the next forty minutes, Benitez and the three other coalition members spoke to the workers. In Spanish, they explained that the minimum wage in Florida was $7.25 per hour, and that the company was required to have time clocks to keep track of the hours worked. "The $7.25 is the minimum," Benitez said. "If you're waiting for dew to dry, it counts as time worked. The same if a truck has not arrived, or if it begins to rain and you have to stop picking but are not taken home." He stressed that the $7.25 minimum applied even if they were working by the piece (paid per bucket). If they picked enough buckets to exceed $7.25 per hour, that was a bonus for their hard work.

What a Full *Cubeta* Looks Like

Benitez then lifted one of the containers that workers use to collect tomatoes onto the table in front of him. Called *cubetas,* the flower pot-shaped buckets are meant to hold thirty-two pounds of slicing tomatoes when properly filled. The *cubeta* that Benitez had put on the table was piled high with bright green tomatoes that were mounded above the rim of the container like ice cream scooped on top of a cone, the way full *cubetas* carried by pickers usually look. Benitez swept his arm over the top of the *cubeta* in the manner of someone leveling a cup of flour. In the process, he knocked some of the heaped tomatoes onto the table. "This is what a full *cubeta* is supposed to look like," he said, emphatically. "There should be no tomatoes in it that are completely above the rim." The workers stood, peered, and began talking animatedly among themselves.

I didn't understand the intensity of the pickers' interest until later that day, when Benitez explained to me that the definition of what constituted a full bucket had long been a source of tension, disputes, and occasionally fistfights in the fields. Workers, he said, run with the filled buckets to a truck and throw them up to a low-level field manager called a *dompeador*, who takes the bucket, dumps the tomatoes into a bin, and returns the bucket empty, along with a ticket that the worker pockets. At the end of the day, pickers count their tickets and are paid accordingly. But it was common for bosses to insist that workers overfill their buckets. The CIW calculated that mounding tomatoes resulted in workers picking about 10 percent more tomatoes than they were paid for—the difference going to the leader of the field crew and the company. Often a *dompeador* would refuse to give a picker a ticket for a bucket he deemed insufficiently full, or would send the worker back to the field to top one up. "It was a constant source of friction and humiliation for the workers," said Benitez. It was also one of the problems that the CIW and growers had to work out. To do so, they met in the CIW offices with an empty *cubeta*, a pile of tomatoes, and a scale. By weighing out exactly thirty-two pounds, they agreed on precisely what a full *cubeta* should look like.

The coalition members also outlined safely policies introduced under the Fair Food Agreement and told the workers
that there would be zero tolerance of sexual harassment—no
dirty jokes, unwelcome touching, demands for sex, promise of
job benefits for sex, or sexual assault of any kind.

---

*As the workers filed out of the classroom on their way to
a day of picking grape tomatoes, the CIW members
handed each a booklet. . . . [It] outlined the new rights
that the coalition had worked for nearly two decades to
bring to the fields.*

At the end of the meeting, Garcia, Pacific's HR boss, stood
up. The room went quiet, and I wondered what he would say.
Would he remind the pickers that they worked for him, not
the CIW? Would he insist that if they did have a problem to
report, that they first approach officials within the company?
Would he give a pep talk urging them to get out into the
fields and bring in the day's harvest?

Instead, he dealt out a wallet card to each crew member,
saying that the cards bore his direct phone number, as well as
the number of a 24-hour employee hotline. Then he began to
speak, slowly and softly. "Call us if you need help," he said. "It
is confidential." He said that the company did not want to
have the abuses of the past repeated. Then he said, "If you see
something, talk to somebody. Tell the guy next to you. Tell
your boss. Tell me. Tell the CIW. Tell anybody; but say something."

As the workers filed out of the classroom on their way to a
day of picking grape tomatoes, the CIW members handed
each a booklet. Printed on thick glossy paper and illustrated
with color photographs, in twelve pages of simple Spanish, it
outlined the new rights that the coalition had worked for
nearly two decades to bring to the fields.

One Major Impediment: Supermarket Chains

Despite the successes of the CIW, there is still one major impediment to tomato pickers fully enjoying the benefits of the newly won rights and wage increase. Although McDonald's, Burger King, and most other fast-food and food-service corporations have signed the Fair Food Agreement, the nation's supermarket chains, with the notable exception of Whole Foods Market, refuse to deal with the CIW. This not only prevents the workers from getting the full benefit of the "penny-per-pound" deal for tomatoes sold to supermarkets (grocery store chains buy about half of Florida's tomatoes), but can leave entire sectors of the workforce without the protections of the moral and financial clout of major buyers pledging not to deal with growers who willfully violate the Code of Conduct. As one CIW member described it, the coalition has built the conduit through which rights and money can flow. Now it's up to the supermarket industry to fill that conduit, if not on its own volition, then with a little of the encouragement the CIW is so effective at giving.

7

Immigration Reform Will Protect American Workers

Adriana Kugler and Patrick Oakford

Adriana Kugler is a senior fellow at the Center for American Progress (CAP) and full professor at Georgetown University's McCourt School of Public Policy. Patrick Oakford is a policy analyst at CAP in the economics policy department.

The nation's broken immigration system allows employers to leverage the immigration status of non-native workers against them, which undermines the employment protections for immigrants and, overall, employment laws for American workers. Unscrupulous employers use immigration-enforcement duties to prevent immigrant workers from filing complaints, lash out at those who seek to unionize or defend their labor rights, or delay or stop an investigation. Passed by the US Senate, the immigration reform bill S. 744 would reduce the role of employers in determining which immigrants are authorized to work and prohibit those with a record of exploitation from hiring vulnerable immigrant workers, as well as improve the mobility of immigrant workers in the labor market. S. 744 stalled in the US House of Representatives in 2014.

Few people would dispute the fact that our country has a broken immigration system. More than 11 million people are living in the United States without legal status, millions of people are waiting to be reunited with their families, and employers are not able to recruit the foreign-born workers our economy needs. But the effects of this broken system extend beyond immigrant workers, their families, and employers; all American workers are harmed by the nation's dysfunctional immigration policies. Specifically, they are harmed because our immigration system undermines the employment protections of immigrants and subsequently erodes the effectiveness of employment laws for all workers.

To fully understand why American workers are harmed, one must first consider the role of immigration enforcement in the workplace and how it affects the employment rights of immigrant workers. Under current immigration law, it is illegal for employers to knowingly hire undocumented workers. Despite this prohibition, unscrupulous employers use workers' undocumented status to avoid compliance with employment laws and deter them from filing formal employment complaints with federal agencies. Many of these employers have therefore managed to go unpunished for their unlawful employment actions.

The enforcement of employment laws is triggered primarily by employees who file formal complaints with federal agencies charged with employment-law enforcement. Therefore, when immigrants are unable to invoke their labor and employment rights, the overall effectiveness of employment laws also declines, as fewer employers are punished for their unlawful employment actions. This means that American workers are more susceptible to workplace violations such as wage and hour violations or unsafe working conditions. Passing common-sense immigration reform—such as the Border Security, Economic Opportunity, and Immigration Modernization Act, or S. 744, passed by the Senate on June 27 [2013]—will fix this problem. . . .

Immigration Enforcement in the Workplace

The intersection of immigration and employment law in the modern era dates back to the Immigration Reform and Control Act of 1986, or IRCA. Prior to IRCA, the United States, like many other countries, relied on border security and deportations to deter and stop unlawful migration. When IRCA was enacted, our immigration policy shifted to include an enforcement strategy located at the point of hire. Congress thought that if undocumented immigrants could not secure employment, people would not migrate unlawfully to the United States. One of IRCA's aims, therefore, was to eliminate economic opportunities for undocumented immigrants through the use of employer sanctions.

In the few cases where employers were fined for hiring undocumented workers, the punishments amounted to little more than a slap on the wrist.

For the first time, all new hires had to demonstrate their authorization to work in the United States by producing documents such as a Social Security Card and driver's license and filling out the Employment Eligibility Verification Form I-9. This form certifies that the employer has reviewed a worker's personal documents that verify the worker's employment authorization. If U.S. Immigration and Customs Enforcement, or ICE, finds that an employer knowingly hired an undocumented immigrant, the employer will be subject to penalties such as fines and potential jail time. Including these provisions in IRCA was significant because it made the workplace an integral part of our country's immigration-enforcement scheme.

While employer sanctions seemed in theory to be a logical way to eliminate the incentives driving undocumented immigration, IRCA's provisions did little in practice to eliminate economic opportunities for undocumented immigrants, for a variety of reasons.

First, the employer sanctions were rarely enforced in the years immediately following IRCA, and employers were therefore only minimally deterred from hiring undocumented workers. Within the first decade following IRCA's passage, the number of employers audited each year peaked at 10,000 in 1990, and the number of employers fined each year never exceeded 1,000. In the few cases where employers were fined for hiring undocumented workers, the punishments amounted to little more than a slap on the wrist.

Secondly, the way in which employer sanctions were crafted created an opportunity for employers to technically comply with IRCA while still hiring undocumented immigrants. As discussed above, employers are penalized if they "knowingly" hire an undocumented worker. But since employers are only required to confirm that documents appear "on their face" to be valid—and many documents can be forged—some employers who in good faith complete the I-9 form still end up unknowingly hiring undocumented workers. Other employers, though, take advantage of this problem and use it as an opportunity to avoid liability under IRCA by completing an I-9 form while knowing that they are hiring undocumented workers. This type of compliance in name only is perpetuated by the fact that many employers and industries rely heavily upon immigrant labor.

Finally, and most importantly, IRCA failed to deter undocumented migration because Congress failed to recognize that workplace enforcement on its own was not enough to halt undocumented migration into the country. For example, IRCA contained no provision for future worker visas. The law ignored the yawning gap between employer demands for workers and the ample supply of such workers in countries south of the United States. In short, it ignored the existence of an integrated, albeit unregulated, North American labor market. In the absence of any new means to enter the country legally, the push and pull of supply and demand led inevitably to more undocumented immigration in the decades following IRCA.

Nearly 30 years after IRCA's unsuccessful attempt to establish a realistic, effective immigration policy, it is little surprise that there are currently 8 million undocumented immigrants working in the United States, a figure that amounts to about 5 percent of the nation's workforce. This large unauthorized population significantly hampers the effectiveness of our labor and employment laws and American workers.

Unfortunately, some unscrupulous employers either use their immigration-related duties or trigger enforcement actions to ... retaliate against immigrant workers who have exerted their labor and employment rights.

A Broken Immigration System Hurts Immigrants' Employment Protections

The nation's employment and labor laws extend to and protect all employees. Since a person's immigration status does not affect whether he or she is deemed an employee under these laws, workers are legally entitled to receive protection under labor and employment laws regardless of their immigration status. As immigration enforcement has entered the workplace under IRCA, however, there has been an increasing gap between the labor and employment rights of undocumented workers on paper and their ability to execute those rights in the workplace. . . .

Employer Misuse of Immigration-Enforcement Duties

As explained above, employers are required to check the work authorization of an employee at the time of his or her hiring. Unfortunately, some unscrupulous employers either use their immigration-related duties or trigger enforcement actions to:

- Deter immigrants from filing employment complaints

- Retaliate against immigrant workers who have exerted their labor and employment rights

- Stall or halt a proceeding after an investigation has begun

In one federal case, for example, an employer who had previously never abided by his I-9 form obligations only started requiring employees to fill out I-9 forms after a union organizing campaign began. The employer, citing compliance with IRCA, fired a majority of the workers—some documented, others undocumented—who were involved in the organizing campaign. Yet the employer only chose to fire those involved in the union campaign, even if other workers could not prove their work authorization. This case is a clear example of an employer wrongfully using his or her immigration-related duties to attempt to deter employees from invoking their labor-organizing rights.

In another reported federal case, an undocumented employee filed an employment complaint after experiencing wage and hour violations. The employer told the employee that he would contact the Immigration and Naturalization Service, or INS—the precursor to the Department of Homeland Security—if the employee did not drop the complaint. The employee refused, and the employer contacted INS, which took the employee into custody for almost 16 months. In this case, the employer, while not required to call INS under IRCA, was able to use his knowledge of the employee's immigration status to retaliate against the employee for invoking his employment rights. . . .

Bad-apple employers who knowingly use immigration-related duties to exploit workers represent the most extreme way in which aspects of our immigration system can undermine workers' employment rights.

In the United States, labor investigations, while usually triggered by a single employee, often rely upon other employees to prove that an employer is guilty of unlawful employment actions. Thus, if employers can create an environment in which employees fear deportation, the employees may be less likely to cooperate with labor investigations, and the employer can potentially avoid liability under employment laws—even if a complaint has already been filed.

To be sure, the National Labor Relations Board, or NLRB, and many courts have ruled that it is unlawful for employers to use or go beyond their immigration-related duties to retaliate against employees who invoke their employment rights. Given that it takes a long time to adjudicate a retaliation claim, however, an employer may still successfully undermine employees' labor and employment rights, despite eventually being punished for their retaliation. An employer can, for example, successfully dissuade employees from joining a union organizing campaign by illegally threatening to call ICE, long before the employer is punished or ordered to stop making such threats. In many ways, the penalty for engaging in retaliatory actions is simply the cost to an employer of avoiding a more undesirable employment outcome, such as a unionized workplace.

Over the past few years, the Departments of Labor and Homeland Security have recognized this strategy and taken measures to lessen the negative consequences of our immigration system on the effectiveness of labor and employment laws. In 2011, the two departments renewed a Memorandum of Understanding, or MOU, regarding immigration- and employment-enforcement activities in the workplace. One aim of the MOU, for example, is to limit ICE investigations in the workplace when a labor dispute is ongoing. This MOU, however, is not a complete solution to the underlying problem. It is simply one way to mitigate the impact of a broken immigration system on our labor and employment laws. The problems that arise from a broken system can only be fully rectified when the system itself is fixed.

Fear of Deportation Keeps Workers from Reporting Claims

Bad-apple employers who knowingly use immigration-related duties to exploit workers represent the most extreme way in which aspects of our immigration system can undermine workers' employment rights. But the immigration system at large also has negative consequences for immigrant workers. Some immigrant employees who are not directly threatened with immigration-related retaliation by their employers, for example, are still hesitant to bring forth employment-related complaints because of the chilling effect our immigration system has had on them.

Research has found that even when undocumented immigrants are aware of their labor and employment rights, they rarely step up and file employment complaints against their employers, out of fear that engaging with the government—even in a non-immigration-related context—will lead to their deportation. Similarly, even immigrants with legal status may fear invoking their labor and employment rights because of how it will affect their co-workers, family members, or friends who are undocumented. One court noted that when employers use immigration-related duties to subvert labor- and employment-law effectiveness, "even documented workers may be chilled . . . [they] . . . may fear that their immigration status would be changed, or that their status would reveal the immigration problem of their family or friends."

Immigrants' inability to invoke their rights results in weakened employment protections for all American workers.

Given how our immigration system has damaged immigrants' ability to protect themselves from employment violations, it is not surprising that undocumented immigrants are some of the most exploited workers in our economy. A

2010 National Employment Law Project, or NELP, study of low-wage industries in major U.S. cities found that undocumented immigrants were nearly twice as likely to experience minimum-wage violations than legal immigrant workers. Specifically, NELP found in its study that 29 percent of undocumented male workers and 47 percent of undocumented female workers experienced minimum-wage violations, compared to 17 percent and 18 percent of native-born male and female workers, respectively. These findings are noteworthy because they highlight significant labor-protection gaps connected to immigration status and gender, meaning that undocumented women are some of the most exploited workers in our labor market.

Immigrants' Lack of Employment Protections Hurts All American Workers

The employment rights of immigrant workers are most directly undermined by our broken immigration system. But the weak employment protections afforded to immigrants have serious implications for the effectiveness of our employment laws and all American workers.

In the United States, the enforcement of employment laws hinges on individual employees bringing formal claims against unscrupulous employers. An investigation or lawsuit against an employer is most often triggered by an individual employee making a formal complaint with a federal agency charged with enforcing labor and employment laws. Thus, it is only through employees invoking their right to file claims that employers are punished for their unlawful actions and other employers are possibly deterred from engaging in similar behavior.

Given this system of enforcing labor and employment laws, it is not enough to simply declare that all workers are covered under labor and employment laws. The workers covered by these laws need to be able to assert their rights in order for employment laws to be effective at securing safe and fair working conditions. Immigrants' inability to invoke their rights results in weakened employment protections for all American workers—and in some instances, means that American workers are subject to violations of minimum-wage and overtime protections, wage theft, and other forms of employment violations, such as unsafe working conditions. . . .

Senate Bill S. 744 Improves Employment Protections

The Senate-passed immigration reform bill would go a long way toward ameliorating many of the issues facing immigrant and native-born workers when it comes to the broken immigration system. The most significant change is the pathway to earned citizenship for unauthorized immigrants, which would provide these workers the ability to secure legal status and remove the threat of immigration action by an unscrupulous employer. Other improvements include:

- Diminishing employers' role in determining whether an employee is authorized to work

- Creating safeguards so that employees cannot be wrongfully terminated due to errors in E-Verify, the government's electronic employment-verification system

- Barring employers who have a history of worker exploitation from hiring vulnerable immigrant workers

- Improving the labor-market mobility of immigrant workers

Legalization

An earned pathway to legal status and citizenship would diminish exploitation by eliminating employers' ability to leverage a worker's undocumented status against them. Workers subject to unlawful employment conditions will be more likely to step forward after legalization and lodge complaints, given that they can receive the full set of remedies and will no longer be chilled by a fear of deportation.

[Under Senate bill S. 744] business owners, when exposed, will no longer be able to hide behind the veil of partial I-9 compliance and ambiguous requirements that enables employers to game the system today.

Moreover, S. 744 utilizes a variety of tactics—from border security to improved employer-sanction provisions—to eliminate future undocumented immigration. One key component of achieving this goal is the elimination of any incentive employers have to hire undocumented workers. . . . S. 744 would extend back pay and other employment remedies—except reinstatement—to undocumented workers. By requiring equal treatment under employment laws, S. 744 will not only improve working conditions for all Americans, but it will also deter future undocumented immigration by removing an incentive for unscrupulous employers to employ unauthorized workers.

E-Verify

Another major component of S. 744 is the implementation of E-Verify. This electronic verification system, operated by the government, minimizes employers' role in assessing whether an employee is authorized to work. Because E-Verify will be mandatory for all businesses, bad-apple employers will no longer be able to intentionally hire undocumented workers and then threaten to use the employment-verification system as a means of intimidation. In short, under E-Verify, employers will be less likely to leverage immigration status against employees as a means to avoid compliance with employment laws.

To be sure, some employers will deliberately continue to employ unauthorized workers by staying off the grid. But those business owners, when exposed, will no longer be able to hide behind the veil of partial I-9 compliance and ambiguous requirements that enables employers to game the system today. If they are not running their new hires through E-Verify, they will be held accountable for deliberately violating the immigration laws and face steep civil or criminal sanctions. This change, over time, will create a strong compliance incentive.

After employer-sanction laws were enacted in 1986, various reports—including a study by the nonpartisan General Accounting Office, now known as the Government Accountability Office—found that employers' duty to determine who is authorized to work led to many instances of outright discrimination. As discussed, under IRCA, employers can be fined for knowingly hiring an undocumented immigrant. The GAO findings suggest that some employers, to preemptively avoid any possible liability under IRCA, used race as a heuristic when determining the work eligibility of employees—by simply refusing to hire anyone with a Latino-sounding last name, for example—instead of examining the Social Security cards, driver's licenses, or other documents presented by employees. Shifting to an electronic verification system may significantly decrease the likelihood of employers discriminating against applicants on the basis of race or national origin.

The Senate bill includes provisions that help ensure that employment and contract rights of visa workers are upheld.

E-Verify is not completely accurate, however, and can occasionally result in employees being wrongly identified as ineligible for work. This has serious implications for Americans trying to secure employment. It is estimated that up to 3.5 million workers would have to visit the Social Security Administration to fix errors in the administration's database, which E-Verify will use. But unlike previous attempts to implement E-Verify, S. 744 has put in place safeguards to protect workers from the system's inaccuracy. Under S. 744, for example, it would be unlawful for employers to fire someone before they receive a final nonconfirmation notice through E-Verify and an employee has exhausted all available appeal processes. The Senate bill also makes it unlawful for employers to utilize E-Verify as a prescreening tool during the application process.

Stronger Protections for Visa Workers

One of the arguments that opponents of the Senate bill often cited was that immigrant workers on temporary visas would harm employment opportunities for American workers. While research shows that this is not the case, S. 744 nonetheless contains numerous safeguards to ensure that employers are not motivated to hire foreign workers out of a desire to exploit them or pay them less than they could an American worker. That is, S. 744 makes sure that employers do not sidestep employment laws while hiring visa workers.

But similar to undocumented immigrants who fear filing claims because of the possibility of immigration-related retaliation, temporary workers who are beholden to their employer for their immigration status may be dissuaded from filing employment complaints. Some employers who have utilized temporary-worker programs, such as the H-2B visa for lesser-skilled nonagricultural workers, have treated their visa workers poorly and in violation of the law as a way to cut down on business costs. The Southern Poverty Law Center, for example, found that despite H-2B workers having a contractual right to earn a prevailing hourly wage between $7.30 and $12.00, most H-2B workers are unlawfully underpaid as a result of "complicated piece-rate pay schemes, underreporting of hours, failure to pay overtime, and making unlawful deductions from work."

The Senate bill includes provisions that help ensure that employment and contract rights of visa workers are upheld. If employers have violated employment laws in the past two years, for example, they are not eligible to apply for the labor certification that allows them to hire temporary-visa workers. This requirement is important because it ensures that employers who have violated employment laws are not authorized to hire more vulnerable temporary workers. Employers who rely on such workers will have a strong incentive to comply with all employment laws.

Improved Labor-Market Mobility

The ability to move freely throughout the labor market is a right most Americans take for granted. But a worker's right to leave a job and find alternative employment creates an incentive for employers to treat employees fairly. That is, if an employer knows that an employee can seek employment elsewhere if they are mistreated, then the employer will be less likely to engage in this behavior in the first place. Thus, improving immigrants' labor-market mobility will reduce immigrant exploitation. This indirectly affects American workers because as the number of unlawful employment actions taken against immigrants declines, a culture of employment-law compliance may be created that will ripple throughout many industries in the United States.

Under the Senate bill, contract agricultural workers are provided with semi-labor-market portability. Workers who either serve until the end of their contract or until the employment relationship is mutually ended will be able to take another job—as long as it is within the agricultural industry and with a certified employer. Labor-market mobility is a small but significant step toward securing better working conditions for these agricultural workers, given that they are not protected by many of the basic employment laws in our country.

Similarly, the creation of the "W"-visa, which allows immigrants to work in nonagricultural, nonseasonal lower-skilled positions, also provides semi-labor-market portability. Like a contract agricultural worker, those in the United States on a W-visa will be able to move freely between registered employers with registered available positions. More importantly, a W-visa holder will be able to apply for legal permanent residency through a new merit-based system. This would ultimately provide the former W-visa worker with full labor-market mobility.

8

Immigration Reform Will Harm American Workers

Peter Kirsanow

A labor and employment law attorney, Peter Kirsanow is a member of the US Commission on Civil Rights, former member of the National Labor Relations Board, and former chairman of the Center for New Black Leadership.

The proposed immigration reform bill S. 744 will harm American workers. The bill is structured to attract low-skilled immigrants and spur illegal immigration, overcrowding the nation's low-skilled workers in fiercely competitive labor markets. In fact, over the last several decades, immigration has accounted for 40 percent of the 18 percentage point decrease in employment rates among African Americans. Moreover, the influx of low-skilled and illegal immigrants will drive down wages for American workers. Therefore, the government must seriously consider the impacts of granting illegal immigrants legal status on Americans' employment and earning opportunities. Passed by the US Senate, S. 744 stalled in the US House of Representatives in 2014.

The Senate this week [in June 2013] begins debate on the proposed immigration reform bill. If this bill becomes law, there is one likely outcome for low-skilled Maryland workers: disaster.

The assurances of the bill's proponents that the bill will somehow help the economy obscure copious evidence that it will wreak enormous damage to the employment prospects of American workers who have already seen their wages and employment rates plummet.

Indeed, it is no secret that the employment picture for low-skilled workers is abysmal. The national unemployment rate has been above 7.5 percent for more than four years, and millions have dropped out of the workforce entirely. Among those without a high school diploma, the unemployment rate in May reached 11.1 percent, and for blacks without a high school diploma, it is more than 24 percent. The Maryland unemployment rate is a bit less grim at 6.5 percent, but the black unemployment rate is 10.2 percent. The labor-force participation rate is at historic lows, and long-term unemployment is the worst since the Great Depression. The workweek is shrinking, as well as wage rates. Barely one in two adult black males has a full time job. A record 47 million people are on food stamps.

The immigration reform bill has the potential to make things even worse. Not only will the bill grant amnesty to 11 million illegal immigrants, it will act as a magnet for future illegal immigration and substantially increase the number of legal immigrants. It is conservatively estimated that the bill will result in 30 million to 33 million additional immigrants over the next 10 years.

Recent history shows that a grant of legal status to illegal immigrants results in a further influx of illegal immigrants who will crowd out low-skilled workers from the work force.

The bill is structured so that most of the immigrants will be low-skilled. They will compete with Americans in the low-skilled labor markets. The competition is most fierce in some of the industries in which blacks historically have been highly concentrated, such as construction, agriculture and service.

Since the supply of low-skilled workers already exceeds the demand, the massive influx in low-skilled immigrants bodes ill for all such workers, but particularly black males. Evidence adduced before the U.S. Commission on Civil Rights shows that immigration accounts for 40 percent of the 18 percentage point decline in black employment rates over the last several decades—the bulk of the decline occurring among black males. That's hundreds of thousands of blacks thrown out of work, who can't support their families without taxpayer assistance.

Driving Down Wages

The evidence adduced by the commission shows that not only does illegal immigration depress the employment levels of low-skilled Americans, it drives down the wages for available jobs. For example, an economist for the Federal Reserve Bank of Atlanta estimated that as a result of the growth of undocumented workers, the annual earnings of documented workers in Georgia in 2007 were $960 lower than they were in 2000. In the leisure-hospitality sectors of the economy, the wages were $1,520 lower.

A $960 annual decrease in wages may not seem like much to some members of Congress, but as President Barack Obama observed when he signed the extension of the payroll tax cut in 2012, an extra $80 a month makes a big difference to many families. It means $80 more toward rent, groceries and the cost of gasoline. Besides, why should American workers suffer *any* decline in their wages because of illegal immigration?

Recent history shows that a grant of legal status to illegal immigrants results in a further influx of illegal immigrants who will crowd out low-skilled workers from the work force. Contrary to the mythology promoted by some supporters of the bill, this isn't because low-skilled Americans—regardless of race—are unwilling to work; it's because they're unwilling to work at the cut-rate wages (and often substandard conditions) offered to illegal immigrants, a cohort highly unlikely to complain to government agencies about those wages and conditions. This inexorably increases the number of low-skilled Americans depending upon the government for subsistence, swells the ranks of the unemployed and reduces the wages of those who do have a job.

Before the federal government grants legal status to illegal immigrants, serious deliberation must be given to the effect this would have on the employment and earnings prospects of low-skilled Americans. History shows that granting such legal status is not without profound and substantial costs to American workers.

Does Congress care?

9

Why Upping the Minimum Wage Requires Immigration Reform

Daniel Altman

Daniel Altman is an economist and author of several books, including Outrageous Fortunes: The Twelve Surprising Trends That Will Reshape the Global Economy.

Employers are attracted to migrant workers because of their willingness to work for lower wages. Upping the minimum wage would increase this attraction, leading employers to seek undocumented migrants in the place of higher-priced native-born workers. The solution to this problem would be to include migrant workers in the labor force through immigration reform. This would allow them to compete on the same terms as native-born workers but without the advantage of working for a lower wage. Furthermore, employers would choose to employ native-born workers instead, who speak English more fluently and are much more likely to remain in the country.

Immigration reform is dead in the Congress, or so says almost everyone. It was the iceberg that caused Marco Rubio's presidential ambitions to founder and just one more crunching disappointment of Barack Obama's second term. But another change in economic policy may give immigration reform new life: raising the minimum wage.

Rationalizing the nation's immigration rules was always going to be a hard sell. American citizens benefit handily from immigration through lower prices for goods and services, decreased uncertainty in the supply of labor, contributions by future generations of immigrant families to national income, and the arrival of new ideas in the market. Yet these benefits are not always well understood—even pro-immigration activists do a poor job of assessing the full value of immigrants and their progeny—and their advocates are not well organized. By contrast, opponents of immigration can rely on visceral prejudices and keenly focused interest groups.

For many employers, a longstanding attraction of immigrant workers has been their willingness to accept lower wages. An increase in the minimum wage for the formal labor force, the subject of Obama's campaigning in early March, may only intensify that attraction. Minimum wages were already rising around the country thanks to legislation by states. Last week, Connecticut's governor signed a bill lifting the wage to $10.10 an hour from $8.70. At the federal level, Obama has asked Congress to increase the rate to $9 from $7.25. In an era in which workers have lost bargaining power through a variety of channels, government has stepped in to bargain for them.

If more employers sought the lower costs associated with undocumented workers, they would probably have no trouble finding them.

What happens when the minimum wage rises? If the new wage is above the rate set by a given labor market, economic theory suggests that demand for workers will fall, that more workers will enter the labor force, and unemployment will grow. In practice, this does not always happen, and some economists believe that higher wages and incomes will actually boost employment in the long term.

Either way, these macroeconomic predictions obscure the decisions of individual households and businesses. In the short term, a higher minimum wage would undoubtedly cause some of them to seek substitutes for higher-priced workers. And for many, the answer may be undocumented migrants.

Imagine a small business owner who has paid the minimum wage of $7.25 to workers since the last increase in 2009. The owner knows that undocumented migrants will do the same job for $5, but so far has preferred to stick with the formal labor force. A jump to $9 would almost double the gap between the two hourly rates, and that's without considering the taxes and benefits that must be paid on behalf of regular workers. It's hard to believe that no one would make the switch, even cognizant of the penalties that could be incurred for such behavior.

But were this to happen on a widespread basis, there would be no change in the number of jobs in the economy. The production of goods and services might not change much, either. The only difference would be who held the jobs.

As the demand for undocumented workers grew, so would the supply. Evidence from the Great Recession suggests that foreign-born workers—documented or otherwise—are very responsive to changes in the demand for labor, despite the best efforts of U.S. Customs and Border Protection. In fact, foreign-born workers even help to smooth out the bumps in the economic cycle, insulating native-born workers from dips in demand. If more employers sought the lower costs associated with undocumented workers, they would probably have no trouble finding them.

In markets where undocumented workers were prominent, a higher minimum wage might actually leave some of the people it was intended to help out of work—though not for the traditional reasons. But the solution would be simple: Get the undocumented workers into the formal labor force.

Doing this would give the minimum wage the effects it was supposed to have. But it's worth asking whether, by greatly expanding the formal labor force, the combination of a higher minimum wage and immigration reform would also increase the rolls of the unemployed.

Fortunately, that seems unlikely. The reason why foreign-born workers are so responsive to the demand for labor is that many don't want to stay in the United States when there are no jobs. It's not as though the risk of deportation is so severe; in fiscal year 2013, only about 3 percent were sent home. Rather, a significant share of migrants come when work is available and prefer to go back to their families and friends when the job is done. This is especially true as the economic climate improves in their home countries.

Of course, as documented migrants they'll be free to compete on level terms with native-born workers. But they wouldn't have the usual advantage of a lower wage rate. Employers would be choosing between native-born workers who speak English well and are likely to stay in the country for the long term and foreign-born workers who might not.

Immigration reform would be a boon to the United States for many reasons, but it has never had sufficient urgency to overcome the inertia of timid and bigoted politicians. Raising the minimum wage might finally give it the push it needs.

10

Immigration Reform Is Required to Protect the Agricultural Industry

Tay Wiles

Tay Wiles is the online editor of High Country News, *a magazine covering the American West.*

Immigration reform is necessary for the future of agriculture in the United States. The H-2A visa program, which currently brings migrant workers to the country for seasonal work, is too expensive or troublesome for smaller growers to participate in, resulting in labor shortages and significant drops in farm productivity. Some growers had expected to hire American workers under the H-2A visa program, but many quit or are uninterested in these farming jobs, which are largely seen as migrant work. A bipartisan Senate immigration bill aims to end the program, streamline the hiring process, and increase the incomes of both migrants and Americans, but such reform is stalling.

When farmer Kerry Mattics sunk several thousand dollars into building a bunkhouse for 12 workers to stay on his property during planting and harvest seasons, he figured the house would be useful for at least a decade. But by 2012, he had no workers to fill it up and his Olathe, Colo. fruit and vegetable farm's productivity had dropped. (They now plant 5,000 tomato plants instead of 9,000 and 7,000 bell peppers instead of 22,000.) The reason: Mattics could no longer afford to use the H-2A visa program that brings hundreds of thousands of migrants to the U.S. each year for seasonal work.

Mattics had originally turned to the H-2A program back in 2008 because he couldn't find enough workers—legal migrants or locals. But, he says, "It just got so expensive . . . (over four years) there were a lot more rules and regulations." For example, when he started taking H-2A workers, he was required to first advertise in Colorado for his job openings, to give U.S. citizens a chance to apply. But now he has to advertise in Utah, Arizona, New Mexico and Texas as well, which triples the cost. A few years ago, he and other employers paid transportation for H-2A workers from the Mexico border, but now, he's been told he has to foot the bill starting at the migrant's home south of the border.

The question of legal labor remains for many [growers] the biggest challenge in keeping up production and making a living.

Needless to say, the fate of worker visa programs, currently being discussed as part of immigration reform proposals in Congress, is a huge deal for ag. Many farmers are still seeing worker shortages because fewer legal migrant workers are available and the H-2A process is too much of a nightmare or too expensive to participate in. (It's worth noting that Mexico's improving economy is likely another reason for the labor shortage. Increasing wages and better jobs in Mexico mean less incentive for workers to come to the U.S. for agricultural employment.)

Nearly 80 percent of U.S. growers surveyed in 2011 said they had "harvest/packing labor shortages." And as security measures ramp up and immigration enforcement cracks down, if the process of hiring workers isn't streamlined, growers are likely to see even higher labor shortages. The West's $68.1 billion yearly agriculture sales could take a hit, and produce prices could rise sharply.

"Mexican Work" for "Mexican Wages"

Some growers have planned on unemployed American citizens taking fieldwork, only to see those workers quit after a few days or even a few hours. Mexicans Mattics employed over the years he says are some of the hardest working farmhands he's ever had, but American workers, he says, just can't or don't want to deal with the physical hardship of working long hours in the elements. With a national unemployment rate of 7.3 percent and over 8 in four Western states, there's still no overwhelming interest in these jobs.

University of California, Merced, assistant professor of history, David Torres-Rouff, says there's historical precedent for this dynamic. "Since the advent of the Bracero Program in 1942," he said in an email, "migrant farm labor has been racialized and re-racialized in successive generations, forming what now stands as an occupation tethered to racial Mexicanness, economic poverty, and the presumption of illegality. In short, migrant farm labor is 'Mexican work' done for 'Mexican wages' in the eyes of your ordinary White American. Of course, migrant farm labor sustains families and nurtures community for those who ply the trade."

Of the crop workers surveyed by the USDA [US Department of Agriculture] between 2007 and 2009, 71 percent were born outside the country. And half of the workers that the DOL surveyed were working without legal authorization.

The proliferation of big box stores that have low prices and that source produce from farms with huge output has made it increasingly difficult to compete for small growers. Yet the question of legal labor remains for many the biggest challenge in keeping up production and making a living. If the undocumented migrant workforce were to be reduced by 40 percent, and Americans didn't suddenly show huge interest in these jobs, producers of fruit, vegetables and nursery products would see drops in output of up to 5.4 percent within 15 years, according to the USDA. The AFBF [American Farm Bureau Federation] anticipated that California alone would see long-term losses of as much as $4.2 billion.

Immigration Reform Is Limping

The political prospect for immigration reform, though, "continues to limp along just as it has for the last few months [in late 2013]," as a *Washington Post* blogger wrote on Thursday. The issue has been hotly debated in Congress since June, when the Senate passed a reform bill that would give at least 11 million undocumented immigrants a 13-year path to citizenship.

"The agricultural sector needs Congress to pass a comprehensive immigration bill to keep farming a viable economic activity in Western Colorado," corn farmer John Harold recently said in an op-ed in the *Montrose Daily Press*.

The bipartisan Senate immigration bill would phase out the H-2A program, or as Mattics calls it, the "paperwork nightmare," and replace it with a more streamlined hiring process. The Congressional Budget Office estimates that the bill would raise income for immigrants and American workers by about $250 for the median American household. "Rather than replacing U.S. workers or reducing U.S. workers' wages, increases in the number of new immigrants lead U.S. workers to specialize in tasks requiring stronger English language and other skills, raising their earnings," reads a recent White House report in support of reform.

But reform is stalled, limping at best. "Immigration reform is still doable, albeit not in as sweeping a fashion as the Senate bill attempted," Jennifer Rubin wrote in the *Washington Post*. Speaker of the House John Boehner, R-Ohio, said this week that the reform won't be in the form of the comprehensive Senate bill, and that it is not likely to happen before 2014.

In the meantime, "maybe we need to find something else to do," Mattics said. "I don't know what the answer is, but it's definitely not going in the right direction for the smaller producer."

11

Agricultural Firms Should Raise Wages and Not Rely on Migrant Workers

Craig Gurian

Craig Gurian is editor of Remapping Debate, a journalism website covering public policy that is sponsored by the Anti-Discrimination Center (ADC).

Many experts argue that the enforcement-only approach to immigration reform, resulting in the mass withdrawal of undocumented migrant workers in the United States, has resulted in a number of negative effects on the agricultural industry, such as increased production costs, decreased productivity, rising consumer costs, lowered profits, and increased competition from imports. However, this argument draws attention away from the real issue: the invisible subsidies gained by agribusinesses from their heavy dependence on an unprotected labor force, who will work for almost any wage. If the real costs of production are much higher without migrant workers, the profits of the agriculture industry must be reevaluated, and other subsidies—created by the government, not individual workers—should be pursued.

A study released earlier this week by the American Farm Bureau Federation on the impact of various types of immigration reform on the agricultural sector wants the reader to conclude that an enforcement-only approach to immigration would mean economic disaster. As it happens, I agree (for very different reasons) that enforcement-only is not the way to go. But the data presented by the study (performed for the Farm Bureau by World Agricultural Economic and Environmental Services, a consulting firm) tells a different story than that which the Farm Bureau wants to tell: namely, that the agricultural industry only survives in its current form thanks to massive (albeit invisible) subsidy from a work force that cannot be described as free, and that the industry must be fundamentally transformed.

The study sets forth a parade of horribles under the enforcement-only scenario. Cost of agricultural production would rise dramatically! Production constricted! Value of farm assets way down! These are findings (note: I have not independently assessed the reliability of methods and data) intended to be conversation stoppers: all good Democrats and Republicans should properly be aghast and join in saying reflexively, "We can't have that."

The argument that "Americans won't do that kind of work" is really nothing more than an argument that (many) Americans won't do farm labor on the cheap.

The study claims, most notably, that the withdrawal of millions of undocumented workers from the labor market would have two impacts. One would be on the general (non-agricultural) labor market, resulting in what the study estimates to be a 4.7 to 9.4 percent increase in the general wage rate. The other would occur in the agricultural labor market. Within agriculture, where the loss of labor from undocumented workers would be concentrated, the estimated change is 62.5 to 125 percent on top of the rise in the general wage rate. The study goes on to predict lower agricultural production, a 5 to 6 percent increase in consumer costs, lower profits per producer, and greater imports.

An Issue of Invisible Subsidies

It's entirely conventional for the study to refer to these changes as cost increases, but there's a better conceptual framework within which to understand them. Ask the question, "What does it really cost to produce food, assuming workers who are not so desperate that they have to accept any wages or conditions that an industry throws at them?" The Farm Bureau study does not pose the question this way, but what it does do—as an alternative method of estimating the impact of the massive withdrawal of undocumented labor—is "look at how much higher farm worker wages would have to be to attract replacement workers from other low-skilled job categories elsewhere in the economy." According to the study, "the most likely alternative for farm employers would be to focus on re-cruiting labor from the construction category," and that "con-vincing the 12% of the construction category needed to switch to farm work" would require a "boost in farm wages to the $20 to $21 per hour range." (Remember, farm labor is sea-sonal; workers cannot rely on 40-hour weeks for 52 weeks a year.)

So, the first thing to note is that the argument that "Ameri-cans won't do that kind of work" is really nothing more than an argument that (many) Americans won't do farm labor on the cheap. That is not something that is widely acknowledged.

Second, we see that what we're really talking about here is an issue of invisible subsidies. To me, the cost of farm labor properly construed is in fact the cost to make that work suffi-ciently attractive so that enough workers who have at least some choice as to employment are willing to do the job. That, according to the study, would "spark a large-scale restructur-ing of the farm sector." But don't we need a fundamental re-structuring if the current system only survives by relying so heavily on unfree labor?

Cheaper Is Not Better

If the true cost of food production—no longer subsidized by a largely undocumented, captive labor force—is higher than it is said to be currently, let's face that straight on. Before we start subsidizing, let's evaluate whether the profit margin in a reformed free-labor industry is really too low (or just lower than producers would like). Before we start subsidizing, let's decide who needs to be subsidized (perhaps a subset of lower income consumers), who should be doing the subsidizing (perhaps the government, not individual workers), and what the conditions of subsidy should be (perhaps a requirement that the crops grown be environmentally suitable for the area in which they are grown).

The data presented in the study does also leave those of us who do want a path to citizenship with a problem to confront. It concludes that a program of legalization and enforcement, combined with a redesigned guest worker program, would have a very different result from enforcement-only: an increase in labor costs of only 6 to 9 percent in the agricultural sector. While better for workers than the status quo, that modest bump for what is, unarguably, extremely difficult work on which we all rely, is only a fraction of the improvement that would be brought about in an environment of real leverage for workers (that is, a relative labor shortage). That is something that deserves serious thought and a sensible response (the most obvious being tightening or eliminating—not expanding—guest worker programs).

One thing is clear: we've got to unlearn the reflex that cheaper is better. Until we do, adaptations to make the kinds of change—in agricultural production and elsewhere—needed to yield a reasonable facsimile of a humane society will remain far out of reach.

12

Highly Skilled Foreign Workers Are Needed in the United States

American Immigration Council

Based in Washington, DC, the American Immigration Council (AIC) is a nonprofit organization promoting laws that support immigrants and increasing awareness of their history and contributions to America.

The demand for highly skilled foreign workers in the United States is increasing, but arbitrary caps in the H-1B visa program do not respond to this changing demand. The competitiveness of the nation's economy depends on the contributions of H-1B workers in several ways. A high percentage of scientists and engineers are born abroad, spurring innovation and job creation; the statistics show that hiring H-1B workers is associated with employment increases. Moreover, H-1B workers fill specialty occupations that do not adversely impact other employees and thus do not steal jobs from native-born workers. In fact, hiring these workers keeps jobs in the United States, and their contributions will become more important as native-born workers retire.

It might seem that persistently high unemployment rates over the past few years have rendered moot the debate over whether or not the United States really "needs" the highly skilled foreign workers who come here on H-1B temporary visas [H-1B visas are nonimmigrant visas that allow US employers to temporarily employ foreign workers in certain occupations]. But the demand for H-1B workers still far outstrips the current cap of only 65,000 new H-1B visas that can be issued each year. In fact, from fiscal year 1997 to 2011, employers exhausted this quota before the fiscal year was over (except from 2001 to 2003, when the ceiling was temporarily increased). As a number of studies make clear, the presence in a company of highly skilled foreign workers whose abilities and talents *complement* those of native-born workers actually *creates* new employment opportunities for American workers. Yet the arbitrary numerical limits placed on H-1Bs are incapable of responding to the changing demand for H-1B workers. This is unfortunate, given that the international competitiveness of the U.S. economy will continue to depend heavily on the contributions of H-1B professionals and other high-skilled workers from abroad for many decades to come.

Foreign-Born Scientists and Engineers Fuel U.S. Innovation and Job Creation

- A December 2008 study released by the Harvard Business School found that immigrants comprise nearly half of all scientists and engineers in the United States who have a doctorate, and accounted for 67 percent of the increase in the U.S. science and engineering workforce between 1995 and 2006.

  According to the study, the H-1B visa program for highly skilled foreign professionals "has played an important role in U.S. innovation patterns" over the past 15 years. This is evidenced by the fact that the number of inventions, as measured by patents, has increased when H-1B caps are higher due to "the direct contributions of immigrant inventors."

- As *New York Times* op-ed columnist Thomas L. Friedman asked in a column on February 10, 2009, "in an age when attracting the first-round intellectual draft choices from around the world is *the* most important competitive advantage a knowledge economy can have, why would we add barriers against such brainpower—anywhere?"

- A 2009 study from the Technology Policy Institute found that, in the absence of H-1B and green-card limitations from 2003–2007, foreign graduates of U.S. universities in science, technology, engineering, and math fields would have raised the Gross Domestic Product (GDP) by about $13.6 billion in 2008, and contributed $2.7 to $3.6 billion in taxes.

H-1B Workers Are Associated with Job *Creation*

- In a study released in March 2008, *H-1B Visas and Job Creation*, the National Foundation for American Policy (NFAP) found that, among technology companies in the Standard & Poor's (S&P) 500, there is "a positive and statistically significant association" between the number of H-1B positions requested by employers between 2001 and 2005, and the percentage change in *total* employment of those employers one year later.

- In 2008, Bill Gates testified that "Microsoft has found that for every H-1B hire we make, we add on average four additional employees to support them in various capacities."

- According to the NFAP, "for every H-1B position requested, U.S. technology companies increase their employment by 5 workers," on average, the following year. For technology companies with *fewer* than 5,000 employees, "each H-1B position requested in labor condition applications was associated with an increase of employment of 7.5 workers."

- This suggests that the U.S. labor market's demand for H-1B workers expands and contracts with the demand for highly skilled workers in general. It also suggests that the presence in a company of highly skilled foreign workers—whose abilities and talents *complement*, rather than substitute for, those of native-born workers—*creates* new employment opportunities for American workers.

- In a survey of 120 technology companies, the NFAP also found that 65 percent had reacted to the arbitrarily low limits on the hiring of foreign nationals through the H-1B program by moving more of their work out of the United States—to countries where the workers they need *are* available.

- A similar survey by the Government Accountability Office (GAO) found that companies which were denied H-1B workers sometimes placed their job candidates temporarily overseas. More than a quarter of research and development centers surveyed stated that the H-1B cap was an "important determinant in the creation of these overseas centers."

H-1B Workers Don't "Steal" Jobs From U.S. Workers

- H-1B visas are issued to temporary, "nonimmigrant" workers in "specialty occupations." As described by the Congressional Research Service, a "specialty occupation" is one "requiring theoretical and practical application of a body of highly specialized knowledge in a field of human endeavor including, but not limited to, architecture, engineering, mathematics, physical sciences, social sciences, medicine and health, education, law, accounting, business specialties, theology, and the arts, and requiring the attainment of a bachelor's degree or its equivalent as a minimum."

- Under the H-1B program, the U.S. Department of Labor (DOL) is tasked with ensuring that H-1B workers "do not displace or adversely affect wages or working conditions of U.S. workers." To this end, each employer seeking to hire an H-1B worker is required to file a Labor Condition Application (LCA) with DOL in which "the employer must attest that the firm will pay the nonimmigrant the greater of the actual compensation paid other employees in the same job or the prevailing compensation for that occupation; the firm will provide working conditions for the nonimmigrant that do not cause the working conditions of the other employees to be adversely affected; and that there is no applicable strike or lockout."

- If DOL certifies the employer's LCA, the employer can file a petition with U.S. Citizenship and Immigration Services on behalf of a potential H-1B worker, who must demonstrate that he or she has "the requisite education and work experience" for the job. If approved, the H-1B worker is authorized to work for the U.S. employer for up three years, with one renewal allowed, for a maximum stay of six years.

H-1B Workers Are Not "Cheap Labor"

- A 2011 report by the GAO found that, once adjusted for age, H-1B workers in most occupations earn the same or more than similar U.S. workers. In addition, the report found that companies hiring H-1B workers incurred significant expenses in fees and legal costs to hire these workers, all of which indicates that companies are hiring the best candidate for the job, not the cheapest one.

- The NFAP points out that employers are required not only to pay an H-1B employee the *higher* of either the "prevailing wage" or "actual wage" paid to similarly employed Americans, but must also pay about $6,000 in legal and government fees for each H-1B hire, plus up to $12,000 more to sponsor an H-1B worker for permanent residence in the United States.

- The NFAP also points out that use of H-1B visas by employers varies according to the demand for skilled workers in general. For instance, Congress raised the H-1B cap to 195,000 per year for Fiscal Year (FY) 2002 and FY 2003, but employers used only 79,100 and 78,000 in each of these years, respectively, when U.S. economic conditions worsened and labor demand declined. If H-1B workers were being used as "cheap labor," as some critics allege, then one would expect employers to hire as many as possible during economic hard times in order to reduce labor costs. In fact, "H-1B filings at U.S. technology companies declined when companies were losing money or hit hard times."

The U.S. Economy Needs High-Skilled Workers in a Wide Range of Occupations

- According to the National Science Board (NSB), the science and engineering (S&E) "labor force does not include just those in S&E occupations." In *Science and Engineering Indicators 2008*, the NSB reports that "about 12.9 million workers said in 2003 that they needed at least a bachelor's degree level of knowledge" in a science and engineering field to do their jobs. However, only 4.9 million of these workers were in occupations formally defined as belonging to a "science and engineering" (S&E) field.

- Moreover, 66 percent of "S&E degree holders in non-S&E occupations say their job is related to their degree, including many in management and marketing occupations."

The Economic Value of High-Skilled Workers Cannot Be Easily Quantified

- The NSB emphasizes that the value of highly skilled S&E workers from different parts of the world cannot be measured in simple, numerical terms given that science is, by its very nature, "a global enterprise" dependent upon the exchange of ideas from a diverse range of perspectives.

- According to the NSB, "new ways of doing business and performing R&D [research and development] take advantage of gains from new knowledge discovered anywhere, from increases in foreign economic development, and *from expanding international migration of highly trained scientists and engineers.*"

As Our Population Ages and Shrinks, Highly Skilled Foreign Professionals Will Become Increasingly Important to the U.S. Economy

- According to a 2007 study by Jacob Funk Kirkegaard of the Peterson Institute of International Economics, the skill levels of U.S. workers are stagnating relative to the rest of the world. As a result, "when American baby boomers retire, they will take as many skills with them as their children will bring into the U.S. workforce." According to Kirkegaard, these demographic trends—combined with the growing international competition for skilled workers—suggest that "in the coming decade, America could face broad and substantial skill shortages."

- Kirkegaard says that to overcome these challenges, the United States will not only have to implement new educational policies to produce more high-skilled Americans, but also "reform its high-skilled immigration policies and procedures not only to welcome the best and the brightest but also to make it easier for them to stay." He finds that the need for reform is particularly urgent in "the H-1B temporary work visa and legal permanent resident (green card) programs."

- Similarly, the National Science Board concludes that, "barring large reductions in retirement rates, the total number of retirements among workers with S&E degrees will dramatically increase over the next 20 years." This suggests "a slower-growing and older S&E labor force"—a situation that would worsen "if either new degree production were to drop or immigration to slow."

American Companies Support American Students and Workers Through Fees, Taxes, and Charitable Contributions

- As the NFAP points out in a May 2007 study, the American Competitiveness and Workforce Improvement Act of 1998 created a training-and-scholarship fee of $500 that U.S. companies hiring H-1B workers must pay for every new H-1B application and every first-time renewal of a worker's H-1B status. This fee was raised by Congress to $1,000 in 2000. The fee was raised again, to $1,500, by the L-1 Visa and H-1B Visa Reform Act of 2004, which also mandated that 50 percent of the revenue from the fee go to National Science

Foundation scholarships for U.S. undergraduate and graduate students in science and math, 30 percent to Department of Labor training programs for U.S. workers, and 10 percent to the National Science Foundation for K-12 math and science programs (plus 5 percent each to the Departments of Labor and Homeland Security for processing costs).

- According to the NFAP, the H-1B fees paid by U.S. companies since 1999 total more than $2 billion and "have funded more than 53,000 scholarships for U.S. students in math and science through the National Science Foundation, as well as hands-on science programs for 190,000 elementary, middle and high school students and 6,800 teachers. More than 55,000 U.S. workers have received training through the H-1B fees paid by companies."

- In addition, U.S. businesses as a whole "pay over $91 billion a year in state and local taxes directed toward public education."

- Companies that rely upon H-1B workers also make substantial charitable contributions that improve the math and science skills of U.S. students. The NFAP notes, for instance, that the Bill and Melinda Gates Foundation "has spent more than $3 billion since its inception on grants to improve education in the United States, with an emphasis on scholarships, science education and innovation in schools." In addition, "the Intel Corporation spends $100 million annually on math and science education in the United States and sponsors the prestigious Intel Science Talent Search Competition for the nation's outstanding young scientists." And "the Oracle Corporation regularly donates more than $100 million worth of software to schools around the country every year."

13

There Is No Shortage of Highly Skilled Foreign Workers in the US

Jonathon Moseley

Based in Virginia, Jonathon Moseley is an attorney, political activist, and cohost of the radio show Conservative Commandos.

The push to grant amnesty to high-tech foreign workers through reforming the H-1B visa program is driven by big businesses claiming to face a worker shortage. However, studies consistently show that there is no shortage of qualified American workers seeking jobs in science, technology, engineering, and mathematics—so-called STEM occupations—and in fact many are struggling to find employment amid layoffs. Still, foreign workers are being imported because they are cheaper. For instance, the Indian government pays for university degrees, while Americans carry high student-loan debts and must continually enroll in expensive certification programs. Rather than turn the nation upside down with immigration reform, businesses should improve their human resources capabilities and recruitment efforts to attract native-born workers.

Amnesty is being driven, among others, by big businesses claiming they cannot hire enough high-tech professionals. These are (or posture as) major donors to members of Congress. So these businesses are twisting arms on Capitol Hill.

Jonathon Moseley, "Amnesty: Not Just for Low-Skilled Workers?," americanthinker.com, February 24, 2014. Copyright © 2014 American Thinker. All rights reserved. Reproduced with permission.

The compromise is that Democrats get amnesty for illegal aliens if business gets more high-tech foreign workers. However, in fact, there is no shortage of high-tech professionals in the USA. Businesses do not need immigration reform.

On August 30, 2013, the Institute of Electrical and Electronics Engineers [IEEE] published a review of this question in its journal *Spectrum*, titled "The STEM Crisis Is a Myth." "STEM" jobs are those in science, technology, engineering, and mathematics.

The IEEE reports: "Every year U.S. schools grant more STEM degrees than there are available jobs. When you factor in H-1B visa holders, existing STEM degree holders, and the like, it's hard to make a case that there's a STEM labor shortage." The IEEE describes itself as the world's largest professional association dedicated to advancing technological innovation and excellence in science and engineering for the benefit of humanity.

The IEEE article continues to the effect that "there are more STEM workers than suitable jobs. One study found, for example, that wages for U.S. workers in computer and math fields have largely stagnated since 2000. Even as the Great Recession slowly recedes, STEM workers at every stage of the career pipeline, from freshly minted grads to mid- and late-career Ph.D.s, still struggle to find employment as many companies, including Boeing, IBM, and Symantec, continue to lay off thousands of STEM workers."

What's perhaps most perplexing about the claim of a STEM worker shortage is that many studies have directly contradicted it.

The Washington Post reported on April 24, 2013, in "Study: There may not be a shortage of American STEM graduates after all," on a recent study by the Economic Policy Institute finding that the United States has "more than a sufficient supply of workers available to work in STEM occupations." The EPI found, for example, that many computer science graduates report that there are no jobs available in computer disciplines.

The *Post* also reported on July 7, 2012, in "U.S. pushes for more scientists, but the jobs aren't there," on high-tech graduates who cannot find jobs. The *Post* quotes Jim Austin, editor of the online magazine *ScienceCareers*: "And yet, it seems awfully hard for people to find a job. Anyone who goes into science expecting employers to clamor for their services will be deeply disappointed."

Shortages Doubtful for Years

Journalists and politicos should have admitted this by now. Back on July 9, 2009, *USA Today* reported in "Scientist Shortage? Maybe Not" the findings of Michael Teitelbaum, of the Alfred P. Sloan Foundation in New York, that there are "substantially more scientists and engineers" graduating from the USA's universities than can find attractive jobs. The Foundation funds basic scientific, economic, and civic research. *USA Today* chronicled high unemployment, drawn from the U.S. Labor Department's Bureau of Labor Statistics, among scientists and engineers in the U.S.

The IEEE article also explained: "What's perhaps most perplexing about the claim of a STEM worker shortage is that many studies have directly contradicted it, including reports from Duke University, the Rochester Institute of Technology, the Alfred P. Sloan Foundation, and the Rand Corp. A 2004 Rand study, for example, stated that there was no evidence 'that such shortages have existed at least since 1990, nor that they are on the horizon.' That report argued that the best indicator of a shortfall would be a widespread rise in salaries throughout the STEM community. But the price of labor has not risen, as you would expect it to do if STEM workers were scarce."

And: "Viewed another way, about 15 million U.S. residents hold at least a bachelor's degree in a STEM discipline, but three-fourths of them—11.4 million—work outside of STEM." Therefore, "If there is in fact a STEM worker shortage, wouldn't you expect more people with STEM degrees to be filling those jobs?"

Most of the IEEE article documents the confusion and inconsistency in the data and terminology, rendering claims of a shortage doubtful. But the IEEE analyzed all of this as follows: "Now, if you apply the Commerce Department's definition of STEM to the NSF's annual count of science and engineering bachelor's degrees, that means about 252,000 STEM graduates emerged in 2009. So even if all the STEM openings were entry-level positions and even if only new STEM bachelor's holders could compete for them, that still leaves 70,000 graduates unable to get a job in their chosen field."

Some computer professionals spend as much as $15,000 to $20,000 per year on certifications and related required courses. Yet high-tech employers want to drive down the salaries they pay.

Foreign Workers Are Cheaper

Okay, so why are we importing foreign workers when U.S. citizens can't find jobs after graduating in STEM disciplines? That shortage of 70,000 high-tech graduates per year in the USA who cannot find STEM jobs gets worse when all jobs, not just entry-level jobs, are considered.

A computer expert working in the field since the 1980s explains one problem to your author: a university degree in India is paid for by the government. So imported foreign workers are cheaper, because foreign governments subsidize their education.

By contrast, my friend still carries $40,000 in debt from his undergraduate degree. So one element of the problem is inefficiency and feather-bedding in U.S. colleges and universities, driving tuitions sky-high—while delivering a lower quality education.

In addition, computer professionals must continually remain current in various certifications in order to get jobs. My computer professional friend explains that some computer professionals spend as much as $15,000 to $20,000 per year on certifications and related required courses. Yet high-tech employers want to drive down the salaries they pay. A professional cannot afford to stay certified on the salaries some employers want to offer. (My friend also notes that some foreign workers arrive with certifications up to date, but their low proficiency suggests that someone else took the test for them overseas.)

The Irrational, Harmful Push for Immigration Reform

So why are high-profile companies pushing members of Congress to pass comprehensive immigration reform, to grant amnesty to an estimated 11 to 20 million trespassers, and also to increase the number of foreign workers who can take high-tech jobs in the USA? Could it be that big, clunky, inefficient corporate bureaucracies are simply not very good at human resources and recruitment efforts? Before reshaping our entire country, shouldn't we first try a shake-up of human resources departments? Before a corporate CEO [chief executive officer] calls his congressman or senator to threaten him, maybe he should try replacing his HR [human resources] director first.

Most if not all state governments maintain lists of available jobs. When one applies for unemployment compensation (your author speaks from some experience), one is required to consult the state's list of job openings. Unfortunately, those databases are widely ignored by employers and badly designed and operated. Perhaps the government should put some time and attention into improving the opportunity for the unemployed to discover that there are job openings.

Instead of turning the country upside-down, maybe we should start with the simple things. Although regulation should be viewed with great skepticism, it would be a very slight burden and a great benefit to require employers to drop a copy of every job advertisement in the mail with a 44-cent stamp, or else send it by e-mail or fax. Since listing the job opening is a free service, the benefit of fewer unemployed drawing on government assistance programs would be worth encouraging greater use of the job databases.

Comprehensive immigration reform is irrational and harmful to America whether we are looking at the low-skill end and amnesty or the high-skill end of the picture.

14

Migrants' Cash Keeps Flowing Home

Miriam Jordan

Miriam Jordan is a senior special writer in The Wall Street Journal's *Los Angeles bureau.*

Despite the unstable global economy, migrant workers from developing countries are sending more money home to relatives. Known as remittances, these cash transfers worldwide increased from $332 billion in 2010 to $372 billion in 2011, with a projected total of $467 billion in 2014. In the United States, cash transfers by migrant workers to Latin America are growing amid a weakened job market, restricted immigration, and border violence. Aside from supporting families, remittances improve economic stability, since the funds are often invested in building homes, starting businesses, and helping community organizations. Furthermore, nations like Indonesia, India, and Mexico were somewhat protected from the recent recession by remittances, which are a key source of hard currency.

Migrant workers abroad sent more money to their families in the developing world last year [2011] than in 2010, and they are expected to transfer even more cash home this year despite the economic uncertainty gripping the globe.

The U.S. leads the world as the biggest source country for remittances, much of it sent home by the millions of Latin Americans working in the country.

All told, the world's 215 million international migrants transferred about $372 billion to developing countries in 2011 compared with $332 billion in 2010, according to the World Bank. The bank projects remittances will reach $399 billion this year and $467 billion by 2014.

For some time now, remittances have played a key role in supporting families and stabilizing the economy of developing countries. Their quick recovery after a temporary dip in 2008 and 2009 has been buffering many countries from potentially devastating effects of the global slump.

Despite the weak U.S. job market, tighter immigration enforcement and violence at the border that have slowed migrant arrivals, central banks in Latin America reported brisk growth in remittances this year. Mexico reported a 5% increase—mostly from the US—to $13.7 billion for the first seven months of 2012. Salvadorans sent $2.6 billion home from January through August, up 7% from the same period last year, according to the central bank of El Salvador. Guatemalan expatriates' remittances, which account for 12% of their country's gross domestic product, also are up this year.

Immigrants who have been in the U.S. for several years are increasingly sending money to their home countries for purposes such as building houses, participating in business ventures or helping community organizations.

The Inter-American Dialogue, a Washington-based think tank, predicts a 7% or 8% increase in remittances to Latin America and the Caribbean this year. The region received $69 billion in transfers in 2011, up from $64 billion in 2010.

Manuel Orozco, the Inter-American Dialogue's remittance director, said several factors are keeping remittance flows especially strong to Mexico, home of the most migrants to the U.S. Washington has been issuing a record number of seasonal work visas for the U.S.: The tally nearly reached 270,000 in 2011, up from 144,000 in 2006.

Educated women are boosting remittances. About one-third of Mexican women working in the U.S. have a college degree or some higher education, and their ranks have been growing. "They send more money than anybody," Mr. Orozco said.

In addition, immigrants who have been in the U.S. for several years are increasingly sending money to their home countries for purposes such as building houses, participating in business ventures or helping community organizations. So-called transnationally engaged migrants comprise only 8% of the total, but they send 10% more money than others, on average, according to Mr. Orozco.

Remittances remain a key source of hard currency for developing countries, often outstripping foreign direct investment and foreign aid. A recently published World Bank book, "Migration and Remittances during the Global Financial Crisis and Beyond," said countries like Indonesia, India and Mexico were somewhat immunized from the global downturn by the influx of cash transfers from their nationals working abroad.

From 2008 to 2009, global remittances slipped 6%, far less than the double-digit slide in foreign direct investment during that period to countries such as India, Indonesia and the Philippines.

"There was an expectation that remittances would fall because of the crisis in countries where migrants work," said Dilip Ratha, a World Bank economist who co-edited the book. "But after dropping during the peak of the crisis in 2009, remittances have not only bounced back—they are at a higher level."

He said many migrants absorbed the setback of lower wages or irregular employment in recent years by cutting consumption, splitting lodging costs and making other sacrifices to keep money flowing back home. Remittances help feed, house and clothe families, as well as pay for schooling and other expenditures.

Intraregional remittances also are on the rise. Migrants are sending money from Russia to former Soviet states, like Tajikistan; from Italy to Albania; and from Brazil to its South American neighbors.

Day laborer Antonio Chavez of El Salvador, who lives in Silver Spring, Md., said he has managed to send his mother money, even when work was scarce during the recession. "I make sure she can pay her bills and buy medicine," said Mr. Chavez, 49 years old. "I'm a carpenter, but I am willing to do any job in construction or landscaping."

Technological advances, such as online transfers with a mobile device, have facilitated and lowered the cost of sending money. Wells Fargo & Co., which transferred $1.8 billion in remittances in 2011, lets its account-holders send money in person, by phone or online through its remittance service. Xoom Corp., an online money-transfer firm, sent more than $1.7 billion to 30 countries last year.

Migrants also are tapping technology to compare exchange rates and fees at different remittance companies. "Migrants know down to the penny a currency's value, and they find the company giving the best exchange rate, fee and service," said Eugenio Nigro, Xoom's vice president of business development.

Intraregional remittances also are on the rise. Migrants are sending money from Russia to former Soviet states, like Tajikistan; from Italy to Albania; and from Brazil to its South American neighbors. "Because of its strong economy, Brazil is becoming a huge outbound market to Argentina, Peru and other countries in the region," Mr. Nigro said.

Of course, remittances could become vulnerable to economic, political and regulatory changes in countries where migrants work. Also, volatile exchange rates and uncertainty about oil prices could have an adverse effect. And persistent unemployment in Europe may worsen migrants' job prospects and harden attitudes toward migrants, creating political pressure to curb immigration.

In the U.S., a new Consumer Financial Protection Bureau rule designed to standardize the remittance industry as well as promote transparency and disclosure could raise costs for consumers when it goes into effect early next year, some experts said.

Daniel Ayala, head of global remittance services at Wells Fargo, praised the rule for creating a level playing field. But he cautioned that, "there are details that could ... ultimately result in limiting access, higher costs and confusion."

15

Migrant Workers' Remittances May Not Help Their Home Country's Economy

Aurelien Kruse and Chandan Sapkota

Based in Washington, DC, Aurelien Kruse is a senior economist for the World Bank. Based in Kathmandu, Nepal, Chandan Sapkota is a former researcher at the South Asia Watch on Trade, Economics & Environment (SAWTEE).

Despite the impacts on household welfare and poverty reduction, remittances—cash transfers from migrant workers to families in their home countries—can eventually become a bad thing for economies. For example, in Nepal, the boom in remittances to 25 percent of its gross domestic product (GDP) has occurred with significant shifts in the trade balance (falling exports and exploding imports), declines in agriculture and other industries, and high inflation. The structural transformations that have created development and growth in other East Asian countries are lacking. Therefore, conventional prescriptions do not apply to Nepal and other highly remittance-dependent countries, and a new narrative for development and growth is needed.

Can a good thing eventually become bad and is there such a point when it becomes too much? Thinking about Nepal's development, remittances appear to be precisely such an ambiguous driver. Strikingly, despite the growing importance of remittances worldwide and its increasingly high level recognition, we are missing a consistent narrative of growth and development for highly remittance dependent countries (HRDCs—a new acronym, for once, may be needed) like Nepal.

While remittances have an unambiguous direct impact on household welfare, the evidence on how they affect macroeconomic variables is mixed. Moreover, their contribution to national well-being is often under-acknowledged in those very countries they support and mixed with a sense of collective shame and fear of dependence. Here, we deliberately leave aside the thorny issue of migrant rights, recently highlighted by a feature story in the Guardian (Qatar's World Cup 'Slaves'), and focus on the economic impact of remittance inflows.

Nepal is an interesting case study. It is part of a small league of countries that receive a significant proportion of their income via private transfers (equivalent to 25% of GDP [gross domestic product]) and the world leader among the ones with over 10 million people.

Leaning against the tide of high and persistent inflows would be futile but simply learning to live with remittances and over-appreciated currencies is a lose proposition.

A bit of history. The migration of Nepalese workers has been taking place for centuries, particularly to India, with which Nepal shares deep cultural and historical ties. In the 19th century, a very specifically skilled subset of Nepalese—the Gurkhas—earned their country fame in the ranks of the British and Indian armies. However, a massive shift happened much later, starting in 2000, driven by both push (the Maoist insurgency in Nepal) and pull (economic boom in the Middle East and East Asia MICs) factors. In 1996, 6 workers left legally each day. By 2013 that number was multiplied by a factor of 200. Remittances followed suit rising from just 1% of GDP in 1996 to 25.5% today.

While the contribution of remittances to poverty reduction is well documented (and striking in the case of Nepal), their macroeconomic impact remains under-conceptualized as well as the ways in which they could affect the long-term growth path of recipient economies.

In Nepal the remittance boom has coincided with a sharp deterioration of the trade balance (with exports tanking as imports exploded), a significant shift in the composition of value added (with services taking up the space left by agriculture and a decline of industry), and high inflation. Structural transformation, at least of the type that made East Asian economies achieve massive development progress, is not happening and Nepal appears stuck in a low equilibrium growth trap.

Ill-Fitting Prescriptions

What do those deep structural shifts mean for developing countries like Nepal that are still struggling to come up with a consistent growth and development strategy for the future? Leaning against the tide of high and persistent inflows would be futile but simply learning to live with remittances and over-appreciated currencies is a lose proposition.

To date, the prescriptions of the development community have been mostly adapted from the Dutch disease analogy, but these appear ill-fitting for HRDCs:

- *Fiscal contraction* to avoid overheating may work in other countries facing short-lived shocks but would not help Nepal, which faces huge public infrastructure and social needs.

- *Sterilization of inflows* has allowed China to maintain a competitive exchange rate; for Nepal it could be unsustainably costly given the magnitude and persistence of inflows. Likewise devaluation could spur unsustainable long term inflation.

- *Tax policies* focusing more on consumption and less on income/tradables could hurt the poor.

More sensible responses emphasize structural transformation to make up for lost competitiveness, but they still appear half-baked:

- *Labor market flexibility* is particularly challenging because large outmigration may contribute to making domestic labor more rigid (low supply, high reservation wage). Is it a coincidence that Nepal has one of the highest average wage rates in the SAR [Special Administrative Region] region?

- *Trade liberalization* may incentivize exports but could just as well annihilate import competing industries, exacerbate the negative spillovers to tradables production and increase consumption of remittance-backed imports. How else to interpret Nepal's huge trade deficit?

- *Investment incentives* may work when the economy is thriving but prove self-defeating if remittances themselves partly drive the poor investment climate (through both economic and governance spillovers). In Nepal, remittances have failed to translate into investment at both macro and micro levels, but they are surely behind the real estate bubble that drove the financial sector to near-collapse in 2011.

We need a new, fitting and consistent narrative. The framework of the Dutch disease (and its resource curse spinoff) only go so far because remittance inflows are more sustainable than resource booms, more countercyclical and less prone to the governance problems associated with state intermediation of revenues (including aid). What we need, in other words, is a "Nepali cure" tailored to the needs of HRDCs. Can you help us find it?

Organizations to Contact

The editors have compiled the following list of organizations concerned with the issues debated in this book. The descriptions are derived from materials provided by the organizations. All have publications or information available for interested readers. The list was compiled on the date of publication of the present volume; names, addresses, phone and fax numbers, and e-mail and Internet addresses may change. Be aware that many organizations take several weeks or longer to respond to inquiries, so allow as much time as possible.

American Immigration Council (AIC)
1331 G St. NW, Suite 200, Washington, DC   20005-3141
(202) 507-7500 • fax: (202) 742-5619
website: www.americanimmigrationcouncil.org

The American Immigration Council (AIC), formerly called the American Immigration Law Foundation, was established in 1987 as a nonprofit educational and charitable organization. The Council seeks to strengthen America by honoring our immigrant history and promoting prosperity and cultural richness by educating citizens about immigrant contributions, advocating for humane immigration policies that comply with fundamental constitutional and human rights, and working for justice and fairness for immigrants. The AIC website includes an Immigration Policy Center that features a list of immigration issues, press releases, and a blog. Publications include *A Guide to S. 744: Understanding the 2013 Senate Immigration Bill* and *Crafting a Successful Legalization Program: Lessons from the Past.*

America's Voice (AV)
1050 17th St. NW, Suite 490, Washington, DC   20036
(202) 463-8602
website: http://americasvoice.org

America's Voice (AV) is an organization that advocates for immigration policy changes that guarantee full labor, civil, and political rights for immigrants and their families. AV works in partnership with progressive, faith-based, labor, civil rights, grassroots groups, networks, and leaders to enact federal legislation to grant full citizenship to the nation's eleven million undocumented immigrants. The AV website features a blog, public polling information, research, political assessments, press releases, and news reports. Examples of the types of publications available here include "New Poll: Latino 'Presidential' Voters on Potential 2016 Candidates and the Role of Immigration Reform" and "Highlights and 'Lowlights' of the Bipartisan Senate Immigration Bill."

Center for American Progress (CAP)

1333 H St. NW, 10th Floor, Washington, DC   20005
(202) 682-1611
website: www.americanprogress.org

The Center for American Progress (CAP) is a progressive think tank founded in 2003 that focuses on a variety of issues, including energy, national security, economic growth and opportunity, education, health care, and immigration. CAP is active in the immigration debate and has advocated for a path to citizenship for undocumented immigrants. The think tank also supports the US Senate immigration reform proposal. On its website, CAP offers fact sheets, articles, reports, and other publications on the issue, including "The Top 5 Things the Senate Immigration Reform Bill Accomplishes," "The 6 Key Takeaways from the CBO Cost Estimate of S. 744," and "Immigrants and Their Children in the Future American Workforce."

Center for Immigration Studies (CIS)

1629 K St. NW, Suite 600, Washington, DC   20006
(202) 466-8185 • fax: (202) 466-8076
website: www.cis.org

The Center for Immigration Studies (CIS) is an independent, nonpartisan, nonprofit research organization founded in 1985 to provide immigration policy makers, the academic community, news media, and concerned citizens with information about the social, economic, environmental, security, and fiscal consequences of legal and illegal immigration into the United States. The Center's website is a source of blogs, magazine articles, and op-eds about different immigration issues, including illegal immigration, legal immigration, the DREAM Act, and the US Senate immigration reform proposal. Recent publications include *Amnesty Bill No Benefit to American Workers; Immigrant Gains and Native Losses in the Job Market, 2000 to 2013*; and *Liberal Voices on Immigration and US Workers.*

Federation for American Immigration Reform (FAIR)

25 Massachusetts Ave. NW, Suite 330, Washington, DC   20001
(202) 328-7004 • fax: (202) 387-3447
website: www.fairus.org

The Federation for American Immigration Reform (FAIR) is a national nonprofit, public-interest, and membership organization that seeks to reform the nation's immigration policies by improving border security, stopping illegal immigration, and lowering immigration levels to about three hundred thousand a year. FAIR'S website contains information about various facets of the immigration issue, covering illegal immigration, legal immigration, labor and economics, guest workers, immigration reform legislation, and population and societal concerns. Publications include numerous reports, an immigration reform newsletter called *Immigration Report*, press releases, opinion articles, blogs, and congressional testimony.

The Heritage Foundation

214 Massachusetts Ave. NE, Washington, DC   20002-4999
(202) 546-4400
website: www.heritage.org

The Heritage Foundation is a conservative think tank founded in 1973 to promote conservative public policies based on the principles of free enterprise, limited government, individual freedom, traditional American values, and a strong national defense. Immigration is one of its many issues, and the Foundation opposes amnesty for undocumented immigrants and has worked to defeat the immigration reform approach contained in the US Senate immigration reform bill. A number of publications on immigration are available on its website, including *The Fiscal Cost of Amnesty to US Taxpayers* and *Immigration Bill Doesn't Secure the Border.*

United Farm Workers (UFW)

29700 Woodford-Tehachapi Rd., PO Box 62, Keene, CA   93531
(661) 823-6151
website: www.ufw.org

Founded in 1962 by the late activist Cesar Chavez, the United Farm Workers (UFW) is the nation's largest farmworkers union, currently active in ten states. Recent years have witnessed dozens of key UFW union contract victories, among them the largest strawberry, rose, winery, and mushroom firms in California and the nation. Many recent UFW-sponsored laws and regulations aid farmworkers. The union is also pushing its historic bipartisan and broadly backed AgJobs immigration reform bill. Its website provides white papers, photos, audio, and video on immigration issues in English and Spanish.

United We Dream (UWD)

1900 L St. NW, Suite 900, Washington, DC   20036
e-mail: info@unitedwedream.org
website: http://unitedwedream.org

United We Dream (UWD) is an immigrant youth-led organization made up of a network of fifty-two affiliate organizations in twenty-five states. The group organizes and advocates for the dignity and fair treatment of immigrant youth and families, regardless of immigration status. UWD seeks to win citizenship for the entire undocumented community and end deportations and abuses. Online, the organization provides information to immigrants seeking to apply for Deferred Action for Childhood Arrivals (DACA) and news about immigration reform legislation. Publications include updates about legislation and court decisions and news articles that reference UWD.

Bibliography

Books

Jeb Bush and
Clint Bolick

*Immigration Wars: Forging an
American Solution.* New York:
Threshold Editions, 2013.

Aviva Chomsky

*Undocumented: How Immigration
Became Illegal.* Boston: Beacon Press,
2014.

Esther Cohen, ed.

*Unseen America: Photos and Stories
by Workers.* New York: Regan Books,
2006.

Nicole Constable

*Born Out of Place: Migrant Mothers
and the Politics of International Labor.*
Berkeley: University of California
Press, 2014.

David A. Gerber

*American Immigration: A Very Short
Introduction.* New York: Oxford
University Press, 2011.

Lü Guoguang

*Behind the Chinese Miracle: Migrant
Workers Tell Their Stories.* San
Francisco: Long River Press, 2012.

Seth M. Holmes

*Fresh Fruit, Broken Bodies: Migrant
Farmworkers in the United States.*
Berkeley: University of California
Press, 2013.

Óscar Martinez, translated by Daniela Maria Ugaz and John Washington	*The Beast: Riding the Rails and Dodging Narcos on the Migrant Trail.* London: Verso, 2013.
Douglas S. Massey and Magaly Sánchez R.	*Brokered Boundaries: Creating Immigrant Identity in Anti-Immigrant Times.* New York: Russell Sage Foundation, 2010.
Kathleen C. Schwartzman	*The Chicken Trail: Following Workers, Migrants, and Corporations Across the Americas.* Ithaca, NY: ILR Press, 2013.
Daniel Sheehy	*Fighting Immigration Anarchy.* New York: iUniverse Star, 2009.

Periodicals and Internet Sources

David Bier	"Low-Skilled Immigrant Workers Are Vital Contributors to the Economy," *Forbes*, September 9, 2012.
William Booth and Nick Miroff	"Returning Migrants Boost Mexico's Middle Class," *Washington Post*, July 23, 2012.
Arian Campo-Flores	"Why Americans Think Immigration Hurts the Economy," *Newsweek*, May 13, 2010.
Bryan Caplan	"Why Should We Restrict Immigration?," *Cato Journal*, vol. 32, no. 1, Winter 2012.
Economist	"A Fresh Headcount," November 2, 2013.

Food Journal	"Immigration Labor Reform: Agriculture Front and Center," December 9, 2013.
John B. Judis	"Immigration Reform Is Labor's Loss," *New Republic*, April 7, 2013.
Mikhail Lyubansky	"Undocumented Migrants Hurt American Economy, Or Do They?," *Psychology Today*, April 8, 2014. www.psychologytoday.com.
Yuko Narushima	"Outrageous Stories of Abuse as Immunity Shields Diplomats in the US from Trafficking Women," *AlterNet*, March 4, 2013. www.alternet.org.
David North	"Is There a Shortage of Skilled Foreign Workers?," Center for Immigration Studies, August 2011. http://cis.org.
Maria Soledad Martinez Peria	"What Do We Know About the Impact of Remittances on Financial Development?," *All About Finance*, September 2, 2010. http://blogs.worldbank.org.
Ai-jen Poo and Tiffany Williams	"House of Horrors: Labor Trafficking in Domestic Workers," Daily Beast, July 18, 2013. www.thedailybeast.com.
Tyler Prentice	"Rotten Tomatoes: Truths About Exploited Tomato Field Laborers," *Undergraduate Research Journal at UCCS*, July 2012.

Martin Ruhs   "Migrants Don't Need More Rights,"
                 New York Times, December 18, 2013.

Audrey Singer   "Immigrant Workers in the US Labor
                 Force," Brookings Institution, March
                 15, 2012. www.brookings.edu.

Brad Wong   "The True Cost of Food: How
                 Immigration Reform Might Affect
                 Agriculture and Guest Workers,"
                 Huffington Post, March 24, 2013.
                 www.huffingtonpost.com.

Madeline   "Filling the Gap: Less-Skilled
Zavodny and   Immigration in a Changing
Tamar Jacoby   Economy," American Enterprise
                 Institute, June 10, 2013. www.aei.org.

Index

L

M

CPSIA information can be obtained
at www.ICGtesting.com
Printed in the USA
FFOW02n0826021115
18217FF